A BOOK OF BEAUTY

THE exceeding beauty of the earth in her splendour of life yields a new thought with every petal. The hours when the mind is absorbed by beauty are the only hours when we really live, so that the longer we can stay among these things so much the more is snatched from inevitable Time. These are the only hours that are not wasted —these hours that absorb the soul and fill it with beauty. This is real life, and all else is illusion, or mere endurance.

RICHARD JEFFERIES

A
BOOK OF
BEAUTY

———

AN ANTHOLOGY
OF WORDS AND PICTURES
COMPILED BY
JOHN HADFIELD

———

LONDON : HULTON PRESS

FIRST PUBLISHED IN 1952 BY
HULTON PRESS LIMITED
43/44 SHOE LANE
LONDON E.C.4
PRINTED IN GREAT BRITAIN BY
W. S. COWELL LTD
IPSWICH
DESIGNED BY JOHN HADFIELD
AND JOHN LEWIS
REPRINTED 1953 (TWICE), 1955 (TWICE), 1956

The frontispiece reproduces
ALLEGORY OF PAINTING
by JAN VERMEER OF DELFT
c. 1665

INTRODUCTION

A BOOK OF BEAUTY—the title begs so many questions that I must first admit how few of them it answers. Let me say at once that this book does not seek to define that indefinable essence which we call Beauty. Although I believe that the words and pictures and music here contained are beautiful, they are not to be taken as criteria of beauty, or as representing the peaks in the limitless landscape of beauty.

It is a partial choice I have made, and a personal choice. It is not intended to sustain an argument or plead a cause. I made it to please myself, and to provide the house of my imagination with a few convenient windows through which I could look out upon life. There is much variety in the contents of the book, ranging as they do from Solomon's Song to *The Young Visiters*, and from a painting in the Lascaux caves to Mr Henry Moore's 'Madonna and Child'. I would not care to specify the common grounds of choice more exactly than by saying that everything I have included seems to me to be illuminated by what Sir Thomas Browne called 'the invisible sun' within us or by the 'fire-folk' whom Gerard Manley Hopkins saw sitting in the night skies.

Since the origin of the book is personal and subjective I must locate its point of origin and indicate the state of mind which it reflects.

Three years ago I fell sick with a treacherous illness which forced me to pass many months in bodily inactivity. I was confronted, as we all are sooner or later, with intimations of mortality. I was also given, as few of us are, time and leisure in which to reflect upon them. Although, at its first impact, my illness stirred up a host of practical anxieties about my means of livelihood and my responsibilities as a husband and a father, I soon realized—as, no doubt, many invalids do —that my dominant impulse was one of intensified delight in the joys of life, in the inexhaustible variety of pleasures which my senses and sensibilities could still enjoy. Life had never seemed so good, so rich in delight. As I watched my normal preoccupations go scurrying by, I asked myself again and again: 'What is it that makes life so abundantly, so triumphantly, worth living?'

In this book I have tried to answer that question. If I had to answer the question in one word the word would be 'Beauty'. That is why the book has the title it has. My more explicit answer to the question, of course, is marked by all the limitations of personal knowledge and taste. It reflects the quirks of a single personality. I will grant, for instance, that the Staffordshire pottery group on page 123 is not as beautiful, as 'important', a work of art as, say, the Portland Vase. It happens, however, to mean more to me, partly because (as readers will observe) the products of the early Staffordshire potters have been a favourite study of mine, partly because I am more readily drawn to the beauty of the commonplace than to the Sublime and Beautiful, and partly because of its unfamiliarity.

Not that I have deliberately made unfamiliarity a criterion of choice. When one comes face to face with ultimate judgements novelty is of no more account than custom. One sheds the whims of fashion. Van Eyck's portrait of Arnolfini and his bride (page 108) has always seemed to me, as to others, the greatest painting of its school and period, and one of the supreme aesthetic revelations of human experience. Familiar though it may be to every reader, my anthology would be incomplete without it.

Nevertheless, I believe that more than half of the colour subjects in this book have never been reproduced in colour before. In the text, no less than the pictures, the recognized heights are offset by unfamiliar foothills. So often during my sabbatical year did I 'see a world in a grain of sand' that inevitably much of the material upon which I drew for this book was not of vast aesthetic scope, but merely mirrored to perfection some restricted, though none the less real, aspect of life. The dew on a spider's web, the outlines of leaves against a stormy sky, the texture of old lace, a squadron of jet-fighters winging through the clouds, a movement of Margot Fonteyn arrested in a moment of time—these are, as it were, twinkling gems in the Milky Way which lies beyond the planetary fire-folk of beauty.

The sentiment of Henry Walton's 'Pretty Maid buying a Ballad' (page 48) seems to gain lustre, not to lose its charm, when placed near Gainsborough's immortal and haunting portrait of his daughters. And the anonymous contemporary ballad which I have printed opposite Walton's picture (and which might, indeed, be one of the very broadsides which the ballad-seller has pinned up above his pitch), for all its artlessness of idea and halting prosody, touches the same chords of feeling as the profound utterance of Henry Vaughan.

Here I should explain the method and sequence of arrangement. In Part I of the book I have sought to illustrate the course of human life, from birth to death, by passages of poetry and prose which are lit by 'a flame within'—if I may borrow a phrase from Dryden this time instead of Sir Thomas Browne. There is no pretension to originality in the theme I have chosen, though there may, I hope, sometimes be a certain freshness of treatment. I have simply opened my 'box where sweets compacted lie,' as George Herbert might have described it, and chosen from it those words and pictures, with now and again a song, which have created beauty from the common experiences of childhood and youth, love, passion and despair, contentment, old age and death. In Part II I have tried to give some indications of the beauty which can be found outside ourselves—in the sight, sound and sense of things devised by nature and art.

Throughout the book I have attempted to weave words and pictures into a coherent pattern which may in itself achieve something of that 'significant form' concerning which Mr Clive Bell has so often addressed us. The juxtaposition of works of visual art and passages of literature—as was ingeniously carried out by Mr Carlos Peacock in *Painters and Writers*, a book which I did not discover until my own was nearly finished—can be a delightful game of aesthetic Consequences. It can also lead to a fuller enjoyment of both forms of art. I pride myself that some of my marriages of text and picture are apt and happy marriages of subject, style and period. I have not, however, made a slavish search for exact and fortuitous resemblances. I have been more concerned that words and pictures should be expressive of the same mood, either by an aesthetic affinity or by an aesthetic contrast. Paul Nash's drawing of 'The Soul Visiting the Mansions of the Dead', though designed originally as an illustration to *Urn-Burial*, is nevertheless perfectly attuned to the music of Vaughan's poem on page 166. It is not to be assumed that the Lady Sophia Pelham portrayed on page 92 had any actual connection with Browning; but as soon as I saw Sir Francis Grant's sombre, romantic portrait my mind flew to 'The Last Ride Together'. And, as it happens, the dates of composition were almost identical.

I should love to go on discussing not only the relationships of the pictures to their accompanying texts but also the deeper, less obvious, 'correspondences', as Swedenborg would have called them, of the works of art and nature recorded in this book to the spiritual and sensual experiences of man. Though I have, through sheer modesty of endeavour, refrained from calling upon Bridges for amplification of my theme, I must nonetheless, with diffidence, put forward this 'box of sweets' as another, if less original, testament of beauty.

It is a box into which all may look, and not only make their own choice, but also devise their own interpretations.

I will end by changing the simile and quoting from another verse of George Herbert's which came into my mind when first I contemplated my task:

> I made a posy, while the day ran by:
> Here will I smell my remnant out, and tie
>   My life within this band.
> But Time did beckon to the flowers, and they
> By noon most cunningly did steal away
>   And withered in my hand . . .
> Farewell, dear flowers, sweetly your time ye spent,
> Fit, while ye lived, for smell or ornament,
>   And, after death, for cures.
> I follow straight, without complaints or grief,
> Since, if my scent be good, I care not if
>   It be as short as yours.

NOTE. *The reference at the end of each passage is to the date and place of its first appearance in print. The spelling and punctuation of the text has been modernized throughout. In order to allow as much room as possible for the illustrations, notes on their sources are printed at the end of the book.*

ACKNOWLEDGEMENTS

THE COMPILER AND PUBLISHERS make acknowledgement of the generous facilities afforded by the trustees of the galleries and museums, and the collectors, artists and photographers, named in the Notes on Illustrations. Acknowledgement is also made of the courtesy of Messrs Faber & Faber in lending electrotypes of the painting by Gainsborough, and Penguin Books Ltd, for lending electrotypes of the miniature by Nicholas Hilliard and the water-colour drawing by Paul Nash.

For permission to print copyright passages acknowledgement is made to Messrs Allen & Unwin and the translators for a poem from Mr Witter Bynner's *The Jade Mountain* and a passage from Dr Gilbert Murray's translation of *The Bacchae*; to Mr John Betjeman and Messrs John Murray for 'Death in Leamington'; to Mr Edmund Blunden for 'The Midnight Skaters'; to Mr Gerald Bullett for two poems; to Messrs Chatto & Windus for passages from *The Young Visiters* by Daisy Ashford and *Disenchantment* by C. E. Montague; to the Clarendon Press for a passage from F. H. Bradley's *The Principles of Logic*; to Messrs Constable & Company and the translators for poems from Miss Helen Waddell's *Lyrics from the Chinese* and Mr Arthur Waley's 170 *Chinese Poems*; to Mr Walter de la Mare for a poem from *Peacock Pie*; to Messrs J. M. Dent & Sons Ltd and the authors for poems from *Tristram* by Mr Frank Kendon, *Deaths and Entrances* by Mr Dylan Thomas, and *Songs and Incantations* by W. J. Turner, and Messrs Dent for a passage from W. H. Hudson's *Far Away and Long Ago*; to Mr Percy J. Dobell for passages from Thomas Traherne; to Messrs Faber & Faber and the authors for passages from Mr T. S. Eliot's *Ash Wednesday* and *The Dry Salvages* and a poem from Mr Louis McNeice's *Collected Poems*; to Mrs John Freeman for two poems by John Freeman; to Messrs William Heinemann for a passage from *Wind, Sand and Stars* by Antoine de St. Exupéry; to the Houghton Mifflin Company for a passage from Lafcadio Hearn's *Glimpses of Unfamiliar Japan*; to Messrs John Lane the Bodley Head for a poem from Mr John Pudney's *Selected Poems*; to Mrs Frieda Lawrence and Messrs William Heinemann for a poem by D. H. Lawrence; to Messrs Macmillan and the Trustees of the Hardy Estate for two poems from Thomas Hardy's *Collected Poems*; to Messrs Macmillan and Mr Diarmuid Russell for a poem from the *Collected Poems* of A. E. (G. W. Russell); to the Oxford University Press for poems by Gerard Manley Hopkins; to Mr Siegfried Sassoon and Messrs Faber & Faber for poems from Mr Sassoon's *Collected Poems*; to the Society of Authors as Literary Representative of the Estate of A. E. Housman, and to Messrs Jonathan Cape, the publishers, for a poem from A. E. Housman's *Collected Poems*; to Her Grace the Duchess of Wellington for a passage from her poem, 'Horses'; to Mrs W. B. Yeats and Messrs Macmillan for a poem from the *Collected Poems* of W. B. Yeats; to Mrs Edward Thomas and Messrs Faber & Faber for a poem from the *Collected Poems* of Edward Thomas.

Acknowledgement is also made to Messrs Boosey & Hawkes for permission to quote a portion of 'Balulalow' from Mr Benjamin Britten's *A Ceremony of Carols*, and for Arnold Dolmetsch's setting of 'Lie still, my dear', from *Selected English Songs and Dialogues of the Sixteenth and Seventeenth Centuries;* and to the Oxford University Press for the words and music of Peter Warlock's setting of 'Have you seen but a white lily grow?'

The compiler also wishes to express his thanks to Mr Frank Waters for his guidance with the musical settings and for having originally suggested the form which the anthology should take.

CONTENTS

PART ONE: THE INVISIBLE SUN

LIFE is a pure flame, and we live by an invisible sun within us.

SIR THOMAS BROWNE
Urn-Burial, 1658

OUR life is short and tedious, and in the death of a man there is no remedy; neither was there any man known to have returned from the grave. For we are born at all adventure, and we shall be hereafter as though we had never been; for the breath in our nostrils is as smoke, and a little spark in the moving of our heart, which being extinguished, our body shall be turned into ashes, and our spirit shall vanish as the soft air, and our name shall be forgotten in time, and no man shall have our works in remembrance, and our life shall pass away as the trace of a cloud, and shall be dispersed as a mist that is driven away with the beams of the sun, and overcome with the heat thereof. For our time is a very shadow that passeth away, and after our end there is no returning; for it is fast sealed, so that no man cometh again. Come on, therefore, let us enjoy the good things that are present, and let us speedily use the creatures like as in youth. Let us fill ourselves with costly wine and ointments; and let no flower of the spring pass by us. Let us crown ourselves with rosebuds before they be withered; let none of us go without his part of our voluptuousness, let us leave tokens of our joyfulness in every place; for this is our portion, and our lot is this.

The Wisdom of Solomon, ii, 1–9

THE SHEPHERDS' HYMN

WE saw Thee in Thy balmy nest,
   Young dawn of our eternal day;
We saw Thine eyes break from their East,
   And chase the trembling shades away:
We saw Thee, and we blest the sight,
We saw Thee by Thine own sweet light . . .

Welcome, all wonders in one sight!
   Eternity shut in a span,
Summer in winter, day in night,
   Heaven in earth, and God in man.
Great little one, whose all-embracing birth
Lifts earth to heaven, stoops heaven to earth.

Welcome—though not to those gay flies,
   Gilded i' th' beams of earthly kings,
Slippery souls in smiling eyes—
   But to poor shepherds, homespun things,
Whose wealth's their flocks, whose wit, to be
Well read in their simplicity.

RICHARD CRASHAW, from 'Hymn of the Nativity',
Carmen Deo Nostro, 1652

16

ADORATION OF SHEPHERDS : PAINTING BY EL GRECO 1608

THE VIRGIN WITH THE LAUGHING CHILD : STATUETTE BY ANTONIO ROSSELLINO *c.* 1465

THE LAUGHING CHILD

HAIL, blessëd Virgin, full of heavenly grace,
Blest above all that sprang from human race;
Whose heaven-saluted womb brought forth in one,
A blessëd Saviour, and a blessëd son:
Oh! what a ravishment 't had been to see
Thy little Saviour perking on thy knee!
To see him nuzzle in thy virgin breast,
His milk-white body all unclad, undressed!
To see thy busy fingers clothe and wrap
His spradling limbs in thy indulgent lap!
To see his desperate eyes, with childish grace,
Smiling upon his smiling mother's face!
And, when his forward strength began to bloom,
To see him diddle up and down the room!
Oh! who would think so sweet a Babe as this
Should e'er be slain by a false-hearted kiss!
Had I a rag, if sure thy body wore it,
Pardon, sweet Babe, I think I should adore it:
Till then, O grant this boon (a boon far dearer),
The weed not being, I may adore the wearer.

FRANCIS QUARLES, *Divine Fancies*, 1632

Andante piacevole

O my deare hert, young Je—sus sweit, Pre-

pare thy cred—dil in my spreit, And I sall rock

20

thee to my hert; And ne-ver mair from
thee de - part.

II

But I sall praise thee evermoir
With sanges sweit unto thy gloir:
The knees of my heart sall I bow,
And sing that richt Balulalow.

WORDS BY JAMES, JOHN AND ROBERT WEDDERBURN
MUSICAL SETTING BY BENJAMIN BRITTEN, *A Ceremony of Carols*, 1943

THE SIGNATURE OF GOD

HAPPY choristers of air,
Who by your nimble flight draw near
  His throne, whose wondrous story,
  And unconfinëd glory
Your notes still carol, whom your sound
And whom your plumy pipes rebound.

Yet do the lazy snails no less
The greatness of our Lord confess,
  And those whom weight hath chained
  And to the earth restrained,
Their ruder voices do as well,
Yea, and the speechless fishes tell.

Great Lord, from whom each tree receives,
Then pays again, as rent, his leaves;
  Thou dost in purple set
  The rose and violet,
And giv'st the sickly lily white;
Yet in them all thy name dost write.

JOHN HALL, *Poems, &c.* 1646

A CHILD

Is a Man in a small letter, yet the best copy of Adam before he tasted of Eve or the apple; and he is happy whose small practice in the world can only write this Character. He is nature's fresh picture newly drawn in oil, which time, and much handling, dims and defaces. His soul is yet a white paper unscribbled with observations of the world, wherewith, at length, it becomes a blurred notebook. He is purely happy, because he knows no evil, nor hath made means by sin to be acquainted with misery. He arrives not at the mischief of being wise, nor endures evils to come, by foreseeing them. He kisses and loves all, and, when the smart of the rod is past, smiles on his beater. Nature and his parents alike dandle him, and 'tice him on with a bait of sugar to a draught of wormwood. He plays yet, like a young prentice the first day, and is not come to his task of melancholy. His hardest labour is his tongue, as if he were loath to use so deceitful an organ; and he is best company with it when he can but prattle. We laugh at his foolish sports, but his game is our earnest; and his drums, rattles, and hobby-horses but the emblems and mocking of men's business. His father hath writ him as his own little story, wherein he reads those days of his life that he cannot remember, and sighs to see what innocence he has out-lived. The elder he grows, he is a stair lower from God; and, like his first father, much worse in his breeches. He is the Christian's example, and the old man's relapse; the one imitates his pureness, and the other falls into his simplicity. Could he put off his body with his little coat, he had got eternity without a burthen, and exchanged but one Heaven for another.

JOHN EARLE, *Micro-cosmographie*, 1628

TAKING OFF

SCARCELY have we taken off when we abandon these winding highways that slope down to watering troughs and stables or run away to towns dreaming in the shade of their trees. Freed henceforth from this happy servitude, delivered from the need of fountains, we set our course for distant destinations. And then only, from the height of our rectilinear trajectories, do we discover the essential foundation, the fundament of rock and sand and salt in which here and there and from time to time life like a little moss in the crevices of ruins has risked its precarious existence.

ANTOINE DE SAINT-EXUPÉRY
Wind, Sand and Stars, 1939

BEYOND our strongest squadron's range
Whom do I envy, O what high prestige
Stronger than gods that still the hearts of boys?
Had I your purpose who affirm a course
With lifting wind, accelerating engines, rise,
I could soar with you in your universe.

Open the sky! So charted are the spheres,
They are as known as calculated days
Or years that mark their passage in a face.
You are impatient for your journey, I
For a sparse house, for living, for increase
Scanted by winter as the growing trees.

JOHN PUDNEY, *Open the Sky,* 1935

VAMPIRE JET–FIGHTERS : PHOTOGRAPH BY RAYMOND KLEBOE 1950

THE MASTERS MARTIN ATKINS : PAINTING BY FRANCIS HAYMAN *c.* 1760

THE SALUTATION

THESE little limbs,
These eyes and hands which here I find,
This panting heart wherewith my life begins,
    Where have ye been? Behind
What curtain were ye from me hid so long?
Where was, in what abyss, my new-made tongue?

    When silent I
So many thousand thousand years
Beneath the dust did in a chaos lie,
    How could I smiles or tears
Or lips or hands or eyes or ears perceive?
Welcome ye treasures which I now receive.

    I that so long
Was nothing from eternity,
Did little think such joys as ear and tongue
    To celebrate or see:
Such sounds to hear, such hands to feel, such feet,
Such eyes and objects, on the ground to meet.

    New burnished joys
Which finest gold and pearl excel!
Such sacred treasures are the limbs of boys,
    In which a soul doth dwell;
Their organizëd joints and azure veins
More wealth include than the dead world contains.

From dust I rise,
And out of nothing now awake;
These brighter regions which salute mine eyes,
    A gift from God I take.
The earth, the seas, the light, the lofty skies,
The sun and stars are mine; if these I prize.

    A stranger here
Strange things doth meet, strange glory see;
Strange treasures lodged in this fair world appear,
    Strange all and new to me;
But that they mine should be, who nothing was,
That strangest is of all, yet brought to pass.

THOMAS TRAHERNE, *Poems of Felicity*, 1903
(written *c.* 1670)

THINGS

AMONG the mind's powers is one that comes of itself to many children and artists. It need not be lost, to the end of his days, by any one who has ever had it. This is the power of taking delight in a thing, or rather in anything, everything, not as a means to some other end, but just because it is what it is, as the lover dotes on whatever may be the traits of the beloved object. A child in the full health of his mind will put his hand flat on the summer turf, feel it, and give a little shiver of private glee at the elastic firmness of the globe. He is not thinking how well it will do for some game or to feed sheep upon. That would be the way of the wooer whose mind runs on his mistress's money. The child's is sheer affection, the true ecstatic sense of the thing's inherent characteristics. No matter what the things may be, no matter what they are good or no good for, there they are, each with a thrilling unique look and feel of its own, like a face; the iron astringently cool under its paint, the painted wood familiarly warmer, the clod crumbling enchantingly down in the hands, with its little dry smell of the sun and of hot nettles; each common thing a personality marked by delicious differences.

C. E. MONTAGUE
Disenchantment, 1922

HEAVEN LIES ABOUT US

Ye blessed creatures, I have heard the call
    Ye to each other make; I see
The heavens laugh with you in your jubilee;
    My heart is at your festival,
    My head hath its coronal,
The fulness of your bliss, I feel—I feel it all.
    Oh evil day! if I were sullen
    While Earth herself is adorning,
        This sweet May-morning,
    And the children are culling,
        On every side,
    In a thousand valleys far and wide,
    Fresh flowers; while the sun shines warm,
And the babe leaps up on his mother's arm:—
    I hear, I hear, with joy I hear!
    —But there's a tree, of many, one,
A single field which I have looked upon,
Both of them speak of something that is gone:
    The pansy at my feet
    Doth the same tale repeat:
Whither is fled the visionary gleam?
Where is it now, the glory and the dream?

Our birth is but a sleep and a forgetting:
The soul that rises with us, our life's star,
     Hath had elsewhere its setting,
          And cometh from afar:
     Not in entire forgetfulness,
     And not in utter nakedness,
But trailing clouds of glory do we come,
     From God, who is our home:
Heaven lies about us in our infancy!
Shades of the prison-house begin to close
     Upon the growing boy,
But he beholds the light, and whence it flows,
     He sees it in his joy;
The youth, who daily farther from the east
     Must travel, still is Nature's Priest,
     And by the vision splendid
     Is on his way attended;
At length the man perceives it die away,
And fade into the light of common day.

WILLIAM WORDSWORTH, from 'Intimations
of Immortality', *Poems*, 1807

INWARD LIGHT

A flower has opened in my heart . . .
What flower is this, what flower of spring,
What simple, secret thing?
It is the peace that shines apart,
The peace of daybreak skies that bring
Clear song and wild swift wing.

Heart's miracle of inward light,
What powers unknown have sown your seed
And your perfection freed? . . .
O flower within me wondrous white,
I know you only as my need
And my unsealëd sight.

SIEGFRIED SASSOON
The Heart's Journey, 1928

THE SENSE OF MYSTERY

IT was not, I think, till my eighth year that I began to be distinctly conscious of something more than this mere childish delight in nature. It may have been there all the time from infancy—I don't know; but when I began to know it consciously it was as if some hand had surreptitiously dropped something into the honeyed cup which gave it at certain times a new flavour. It gave me little thrills, often purely pleasureable, at other times startling, and there were occasions when it became so poignant as to frighten me. The sight of a magnificent sunset was sometimes almost more than I could endure and made me wish to hide myself away. But when the feeling was roused by the sight of a small and beautiful or singular object, such as a flower, its sole effect was to intensify the object's loveliness . . .

The feeling, however, was evoked more powerfully by trees than by even the most supernatural of my flowers; it varied in power according to time and place and the appearance of the tree or trees, and always affected me most on moonlight nights. Frequently, after I had first begun to experience it consciously, I would go out of my way to meet it, and I used to steal out of the house alone when the moon was at its full to stand, silent and motionless, near some group of large trees, gazing at the dusky green foliage silvered by the beams; and at such times the sense of mystery would grow until a sensation of delight would change to fear, and the fear increase until it was no longer to be borne, and I would hastily escape to recover the sense of reality and safety indoors, where there was light and company.

W. H. HUDSON
Far Away and Long Ago, 1918

IMMORTAL WHEAT

THE corn was orient and immortal wheat, which never should be reaped, nor was ever sown. I thought it had stood from everlasting to everlasting. The dust and stones of the street were as precious as gold; the gates were at first the end of the world. The green trees, when I saw them first through one of the gates, transported and ravished me: their sweetness and unusual beauty made my heart to leap, and almost mad with ecstasy, they were such strange and wonderful things. The Men! O what venerable and reverend creatures did the aged seem! Immortal Cherubims! And young men glittering and sparkling Angels, and maids strange seraphic pieces of life and beauty! Boys and girls, tumbling in the street and playing, were moving jewels. I knew not that they were born or should die; but all things abided eternally as they were in their proper places. Eternity was manifest in the light of the day, and something infinite behind everything appeared, which talked with my expectation and moved my desire. The city seemed to stand in Eden, or to be built in Heaven. The streets were mine, the temple was mine, the people were mine, their clothes and gold and silver were mine, as much as their sparkling eyes, fair skins and ruddy faces. The skies were mine, and so were the sun and moon and stars; and all the World was mine, and I the only spectator and enjoyer of it. I knew no churlish proprieties nor bounds, nor divisions: but all proprieties and divisions were mine; all treasures and the possessors of them.

THOMAS TRAHERNE, *Centuries of Meditations*,
1908 (written *c.* 1670)

SUMMER : FROM THE FOUR SEASONS
DETAIL OF SHELDON TAPESTRY, 1611

A HORSEMAN : STAFFORDSHIRE SALT-GLAZE POTTERY FIGURE *c.* 1740

UNCLE TOBY ON HIS HOBBY-HORSE

IF, when I was a school-boy, I could not hear a drum beat, but my heart beat with it—was it my fault? Did I plant the propensity there?—Did I sound the alarm within, or Nature? . . . When we read over the siege of *Troy*, which lasted ten years and eight months —though with such a train of artillery as we had at *Namur*, the town might have been carried in a week—was I not as concerned for the destruction of the *Greeks* and *Trojans* as any boy of the whole school? Had I not three strokes of a ferula given me, two on my right hand, and one on my left, for calling *Helena* a bitch for it? Did any one of you shed more tears for *Hector?* And when king *Priam* came to the camp to beg his body, and returned weeping back to *Troy* without it—you know, brother, I could not eat my dinner. Did that bespeak me cruel? Or because, brother Shandy, my blood flew out into the camp, and my heart panted for war—was it a proof it could not ache for the distresses of war too? O brother! 'tis one thing for a soldier to gather laurels—and 'tis another to scatter cypress . . . For what is war? What is it, Yorick, when fought as ours has been, upon principles of *liberty*, and upon principles of *honour*—what is it, but the getting together of quiet and harmless people, with their swords in their hands, to keep the ambitious and the turbulent within bounds? And heaven is my witness, brother Shandy, that the pleasure I have taken in these things—and that infinite delight, in particular, which has attended my sieges in my bowling-green, has arose within me, and I hope in the corporal too, from the consciousness we both had, that in carrying them on, we were answering the great ends of our creation.

LAURENCE STERNE
Tristram Shandy, Book VI, 1762

37

MORNING

I went to the window, where the morning was,
And saw innocence scattered on the grass.
On blade and bough it lay, on wall and gable,
Fresh with the freshness of old fable.

A blackbird on the lawn stood listening,
His orange beak glistening,
His every feather still as stone.
Such stillness, such brightness, I had never known.

Still was the garden, and, beyōnd,
The frosted pane of the duck-pond.
And quilted downs and distant cottages
Stood not more still than the austere trees.

Morning, new-born of a pale, virgin sky,
Found those bare trees as much surprised as I.
But though I stared and stared, and stare my fill,
They keep their secret, still.

GERALD BULLETT
'White Frost', *Poems in Pencil*, 1937

IDLE DIVERSIONS

I TOLD how good she was to all her grandchildren, having us to the great house in the holidays, where I in particular used to spend many hours by myself, in gazing upon the old busts of the twelve Caesars, that had been Emperors of Rome, till the old marble heads would seem to live again, or I to be turned into marble with them; how I never could be tired with roaming about that huge mansion, with its vast empty rooms, with their worn-out hangings, fluttering tapestry, and carved oaken panels, with the gilding almost rubbed out; sometimes in the spacious old-fashioned gardens, which I had almost to myself, unless when now and then a solitary gardening man would cross me; and how the nectarines and peaches hung upon the walls, without my ever offering to pluck them, because they were forbidden fruit, unless now and then—and because I had more pleasure in strolling about among the old melancholy looking yew-trees or the firs, and picking up the red berries and the fir-apples, which were good for nothing but to look at, or in lying about upon the fresh grass with all the fine garden smells around me, or basking in the orangery, till I could almost fancy myself ripening too along with the oranges and the limes in that grateful warmth, or in watching the dace that darted to and fro in the fish-pond at the bottom of the garden, with here and there a great sulky pike hanging midway down the water in silent state, as if it mocked at their impertinent friskings. I had more pleasure in these busy-idle diversions than in all the sweet flavours of peaches, nectarines, oranges, and such-like common baits of children.

CHARLES LAMB
From 'Dream Children', *Elia*, 1823

ANGEL-INFANCY

HAPPY those early days, when I
Shined in my angel-infancy!
Before I understood this place
Appointed for my second race,
Or taught my soul to fancy aught
But a white, celestial thought:
When yet I had not walked above
A mile or two from my first love,
And looking back—at that short space—
Could see a glimpse of His bright face:
When on some gilded cloud, or flower,
My gazing soul would dwell an hour,
And in those weaker glories spy
Some shadows of eternity:
Before I taught my tongue to wound
My conscience with a sinful sound,
Or had the black art to dispense
A several sin to every sense,
But felt through all this fleshly dress
Bright shoots of everlastingness.

HENRY VAUGHAN, from 'The Retreat'
Silex Scintillans, 1650

THE PAINTER'S DAUGHTERS : PAINTING BY THOMAS GAINSBOROUGH *c.* 1760

A MILKMAID : STAFFORDSHIRE POTTERY GROUP *c.* 1755

A FAIR AND HAPPY MILKMAID

ALL her excellencies stand in her so silently, as if they had stolen upon her without her knowledge. The lining of her apparel (which is her self) is far better than outsides of tissue; for though she be not arrayed in the spoil of the silk-worm, she is decked in innocence, a far better wearing. She doth not, with lying long abed, spoil both her complexion and conditions; nature hath taught her too immoderate sleep is rust to the soul: she rises therefore with Chanticlere, her dame's cock, and at night makes the lamb her curfew. In milking a cow, and straining the teats through her fingers, it seems that so sweet a milk-press makes the milk the whiter or sweeter; for never came almond glove or aromatic ointment on her palm to taint it. The golden ears of corn fall and kiss her feet when she reaps them, as if they wished to be bound and led prisoners by the same hand [that] felled them. Her breath is her own, which scents all the year long of June, like a new-made haycock. She makes her hand hard with labour, and her heart soft with pity; and when winter evenings fall early (sitting at her merry wheel) she sings a defiance to the giddy wheel of Fortune. She doth all things with so sweet a grace, it seems ignorance will not suffer her to do ill . . . Thus lives she, and all her care is, she may die in the springtime, to have store of flowers upon her winding sheet.

SIR THOMAS OVERBURY, *New Characters*, 1615

THE QUESTION

I dreamed that, as I wandered by the way,
  Bare Winter suddenly was changed to Spring;
And gentle odours led my steps astray,
  Mixed with a sound of waters murmuring
Along a shelving bank of turf, which lay
  Under a copse, and hardly dared to fling
Its green arms round the bosom of the stream,
But kissed it and then fled, as thou mightest in dream.

There grew pied wind-flowers and violets;
  Daisies, those pearled Arcturi of the earth,
The constellated flower that never sets;
  Faint oxlips; tender bluebells, at whose birth
The sod scarce heaved; and that tall flower that wets—
  Like a child, half in tenderness and mirth—
Its mother's face with Heaven's collected tears
When the low wind, its playmate's voice, it hears.

And in the warm hedge grew lush eglantine,
  Green cowbind and the moonlight-coloured may
And cherry-blossoms, and white cups whose wine
  Was the bright dew yet drained not by the day;
And wild roses, and ivy serpentine,
  With its dark buds and leaves wandering astray;
And flowers, azure, black, and streaked with gold,
Fairer than any wakened eyes behold.

And nearer to the river's trembling edge
    There grew broad flag-flowers, purple pranked with white,
And starry river-buds among the sedge,
    And floating water-lilies, broad and bright,
Which lit the oak that overhung the hedge
    With moonlight beams of their own watery light;
And bulrushes, and reeds of such deep green
As soothed the dazzled eye with sober sheen.

Methought that of these visionary flowers
    I made a nosegay, bound in such a way
That the same hues which in their natural bowers
    Were mingled or opposed, the like array
Kept these imprisoned children of the Hours
    Within my hand;—and then, elate and gay,
I hastened to the spot whence I had come,
That I might there present it—O! to whom?

PERCY BYSSHE SHELLEY
in *The Literary Pocket-Book*, 1822

THE PROMISE OF SPRING

NOT in those climes where I have late been straying,
Though Beauty long hath there been matchless deemed;
Not in those visions to the heart displaying
Forms which it sighs but to have only dreamed,
Hath aught like thee in truth or fancy seemed:
Nor, having seen thee, shall I vainly seek
To paint those charms which varied as they beamed—
To such as see thee not my words were weak;
To those who gaze on thee what language could they speak?

Ah! may'st thou ever be what now thou art,
Nor unbeseem the promise of thy spring,
As fair in form, as warm yet pure in heart,
Love's image upon earth without his wing,
And guileless beyond Hope's imagining!
And surely she who now so fondly rears
Thy youth, in thee, thus hourly brightening,
Beholds the rainbow of her future years,
Before whose heavenly hues all sorrow disappears . . .

GEORGE GORDON, BARON BYRON
'To Ianthe. A Dedication'
Childe Harold's Pilgrimage, 1812

A GIRL SEWING : DRAWING BY JEAN ANTOINE WATTEAU *c.* 1710

A PRETTY MAID BUYING A BALLAD : PAINTING BY HENRY WALTON 1778

THE MAIDEN'S LAMENT

ONE morning very early, one morning in the spring,
I heard a maid in Bedlam who mournfully did sing,
Her chains she rattled on her hands while sweetly thus sung she,
I love my love, because I know my love loves me.

Oh cruel were his parents who sent my love to sea,
And cruel cruel was the ship that bore my love from me,
Yet I love his parents since they're his, although they've ruined me,
And I love my love, because I know my love loves me.

Oh should it please the pitying powers to call me to the sky,
I'd claim a guardian angel's charge around my love to fly;
To guard him from all dangers how happy should I be!
For I love my love, because I know my love loves me.

I'll make a strawy garland, I'll make it wondrous fine,
With roses, lilies, daisies, I'll mix the eglantine;
And I'll present it to my love when he returns from sea,
For I love my love, because I know my love loves me.

Oh if I were a little bird to build upon his breast,
Or if I were a nightingale to sing my love to rest!
To gaze upon his lovely eyes all my reward should be;
For I love my love, because I know my love loves me.

Oh if I were an eagle, to soar into the sky!
I'd gaze around with piercing eyes where I my love might spy;
But ah! unhappy maiden, that love you ne'er shall see,
Yet I love my love, because I know my love loves me.

ANONYMOUS, Eighteenth-century ballad
in John Aikin's *Essays on Song-Writing*, 1774

A PROPOSALE

SHE looked very beautifull with some red roses in her hat and the dainty red ruge in her cheeks looked quite the thing. Bernard heaved a sigh and his eyes flashed as he beheld her and Ethel thorght to herself what a fine type of manhood he reprisented with his nice thin legs in pale broun trousers and well fitting spats and a red rose in his button hole and rarther a sporting cap which gave him a great air with its quaint check and little flaps to pull down if necessary. Off they started the envy of all the waiters.

They arrived at Windsor very hot from the jorney and Bernard at once hired a boat to row his beloved up the river. Ethel could not row but she much enjoyed seeing the tough sunburnt arms of Bernard tugging at the oars as she lay among the rich cushons of the dainty boat. She had a rarther lazy nature but Bernard did not know of this. However he soon got dog tired and sugested lunch by the mossy bank.

O yes said Ethel quickly opening the sparkling champaigne.

Dont spill any cried Bernard as he carved some chicken.

They eat and drank deeply of the charming viands ending up with merangs and choclates.

Let us now bask under the spreading trees said Bernard in a passiunate tone.

Oh yes lets said Ethel and she opened her dainty parasole and sank down upon the long green grass. She closed her eyes but she was far from asleep. Bernard sat beside her in profound silence gazing at her pink face and long wavy eye lashes. He puffed at his pipe for some moments while the larks gaily caroled in the blue sky. Then he edged a trifle closer to Ethels form.

Ethel he murmered in a trembly voice.

Oh what is it said Ethel hastily sitting up.

Words fail me ejaculated Bernard horsly my passion for you is intense he added fervently. It has grown day and night since I first beheld you.

Oh said Ethel in supprise I am not prepared for this and she lent back against the trunk of the tree.

Bernard placed one arm tightly round her. When will you marry me Ethel he uttered you must be my wife it has come to that I love you so intensly that if you say no I shall perforce dash my body to the brink of yon muddy river he panted wildly.

Oh dont do that implored Ethel breathing rarther hard.

Then say you love me he cried.

Oh Bernard she sighed fervently I certinly love you madly you are to me like a Heathen god she cried looking at his manly form and handsome flashing face I will indeed marry you.

How soon gasped Bernard gazing at her intensly.

As soon as possible said Ethel gently closing her eyes.

My Darling whispered Bernard and he seized her in his arms we will be marrid next week.

Oh Bernard muttered Ethel this is so sudden.

DAISY ASHFORD (written at the age of nine years)
The Young Visiters, 1919

WORDS BY BEN JONSON 1616

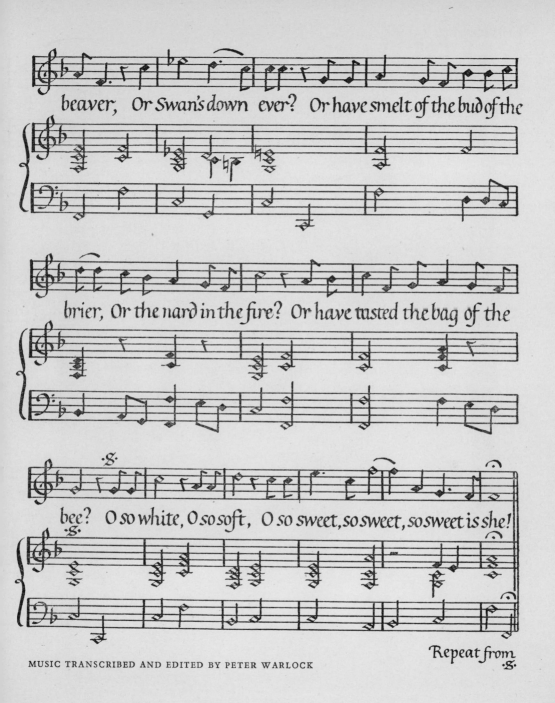

beaver, Or Swan's down ever? Or have smelt of the bud of the

brier, Or the nard in the fire? Or have tasted the bag of the

bee? O so white, O so soft, O so sweet, so sweet, so sweet is she!

MUSIC TRANSCRIBED AND EDITED BY PETER WARLOCK

LOVE BADE ME WELCOME

Love bade me welcome; yet my soul drew back,
    Guilty of dust and sin.
But quick-eyed Love, observing me grow slack
    From my first entrance in,
Drew nearer to me, sweetly questioning
    If I lacked anything.

'A guest,' I answered, 'worthy to be here:'
    Love said, 'You shall be he'.
'I, the unkind, ungrateful? Ah, my dear,
    I cannot look on Thee'.
Love took my hand, and smiling did reply,
    'Who made the eyes but I?'

'Truth, Lord; but I have marred them: let my shame
    Go where it doth deserve'.
'And know you not,' says Love, 'Who bore the blame?'
    'My dear, then I will serve'.
'You must sit down,' says Love, 'and taste my meat'.
    So I did sit and eat.

GEORGE HERBERT, *The Temple*, 1633

THE DAWNING

AH! what time wilt thou come? when shall that cry
'The Bridegroom's coming!' fill the sky?
Shall it in the evening run
When our words and works are done?
Or will thy all-surprising light
    Break at midnight,
When either sleep, or some dark pleasure
Possesseth mad man without measure?
Or shall these early, fragrant hours
    Unlock thy bowers?
And with their blush of light descry
Thy locks crowned with eternity?
Indeed, it is the only time
That with thy glory doth best chime;
All now are stirring, every field
    Full hymns doth yield;
The whole Creation shakes off night,
And for thy shadow looks the light;
Stars now vanish without number,
Sleepy planets set and slumber,
The pursy clouds disband and scatter,
All expect some sudden matter;
Not one beam triumphs, but from far
    That morning-star . . .

HENRY VAUGHAN, *Silex Scintillans,* 1650

SLEEPING BEAUTY

Thus lovely, sleep did first appear,
    Ere yet it was with death allied,
When the first fair one, like her here,
    Lay down, and for a little died.

Ere happy souls knew how to die,
    And trod the rougher paths to bliss,
Transported in an ecstasy,
    They breathed out such smooth ways as this.

Her hand bears gently up her head,
    And, like a pillow, raised does keep,
But softer than her couch is spread,
    Though that be softer than her sleep.

Alas! that death-like sleep, or night,
    Should power have to close those eyes,
Which once vied with the fairest light
    Or what gay colours thence did rise.

Ah! that lost beams thus long have shined
    To them with darkness over-spread,
Unseen, as day breaks, to the blind,
    Or the sun rises, to the dead.

That sun, in all his eastern pride,
    Did never see a shape so rare
Nor night within its black arms hide
    A silent beauty half so fair.

RICHARD LEIGH, *Poems*, 1675

JUPITER AND ANTIOPE : PAINTING BY CORREGGIO c. 1522

FOURTEENTH-CENTURY FRENCH IVORY MIRROR CASE

THE COMING OF SPRING

My beloved spake, and said unto me, Rise up, my love, my fair one, and come away. For, lo, the winter is past, the rain is over and gone; the flowers appear on the earth; the time of the singing of birds is come, and the voice of the turtle is heard in our land; the fig tree putteth forth her green figs, and the vines with the tender grape give a good smell. Arise, my love, my fair one, and come away.

Solomon's Song, ii, 10-13

WHAT is all this juice and all this joy?
A strain of the earth's sweet being in the beginning
In Eden garden.

GERARD MANLEY HOPKINS

LOVE IN SECRET

I hid my love when young till I
Couldn't bear the buzzing of a fly;
I hid my love to my despite
Till I could not bear to look at light:
I dare not gaze upon her face
But left her memory in each place;
Where'er I saw a wild flower lie
I kissed and bade my love good-bye.

I met her in the greenest dells,
Where dewdrops pearl the wood bluebells;
The lost breeze kissed her bright blue eye,
The bee kissed and went singing by,
A sunbeam found a passage there,
A gold chain round her neck so fair;
As secret as the wild bee's song
She lay there all the summer long.

I hid my love in field and town
Till e'en the breeze would knock me down;
The bees seemed singing ballads o'er,
The fly's bass turned a lion's roar;
And even silence found a tongue
To haunt me all the summer long;
The riddle nature could not prove
Was nothing else but secret love.

JOHN CLARE, *Poems,* 1920
(written *c.* 1860)

60

LOVE IN STATE

So she furnished herself with a world of gifts, store of gold and silver, and of riches . . . But yet she carried nothing with her wherein she trusted more than in herself, and in the charms and enchantment of her passing beauty and grace. Therefore when she was sent unto by divers letters . . . she mocked Antonius so much that she disdained to set forward otherwise, but to take her barge in the river of Cydnus; the poop whereof was of gold, the sails of purple, and the oars of silver, which kept stroke in rowing after the sound of the music of flutes, howboys, citherns, viols, and such other instruments as they played upon in the barge. And now for the person of herself: she was laid under a pavilion of cloth of gold of tissue, apparelled and attired like the goddess Venus commonly drawn in picture: and hard by her, on either hand of her, pretty fair boys apparelled as painters do set forth god Cupid, with little fans in their hands, with the which they fanned wind upon her. Her Ladies and Gentlewomen also, the fairest of them were apparelled like the nymphs Nereids (which are the Mermaids of the waters) and like the Graces, some steering the helm, others tending the tackle and ropes of the barge, out of the which there came a wonderful passing sweet savour of perfumes, that perfumed the wharf's side, pestered with innumerable multitudes of people. Some of them followed the barge all alongst the river-side: others also ran out of the city to see her coming in. So that in the end there ran such multitudes of people one after another to see her, that Antonius was left post alone in the market-place in his Imperial seat to give audience: and there went a rumour in the people's mouths, that the goddess Venus was come to play with the god Bacchus.

PLUTARCH, *Lives of the Noble Grecians and Romans*, translated by Sir Thomas North, 1579

EGYPTIAN VENUS

THE barge she sat in, like a burnished throne,
Burned on the water: the poop was beaten gold;
Purple the sails, and so perfumëd that
The winds were love-sick with them: the oars were silver,
Which to the tune of flutes kept stroke, and made
The water which they beat to follow faster,
As amorous of their strokes. For her own person
It beggared all description: she did lie
In her pavilion, cloth-of-gold of tissue,
O'erpicturing that Venus where we see
The fancy out-work nature: on each side her,
Stood pretty, dimpled boys, like smiling Cupids,
With divers-coloured fans, whose wind did seem
To glow the delicate cheeks which they did cool,
And what they undid, did . . .
　　Her gentlewomen, like the Nereides,
So many mermaids, tended her i' the eyes,
And made their bends adornings: at the helm
A seeming mermaid steers: the silken tackle
Swells with the touches of those flower-soft hands,
That yarely frame the office. From the barge
A strange invisible perfume hits the sense
Of the adjacent wharfs. The city cast
Her people out upon her; and Antony,
Enthroned i' the market-place, did sit alone,
Whistling to the air, which, but for vacancy,
Had gone to gaze on Cleopatra too,
And made a gap in nature.

WILLIAM SHAKESPEARE, *Antony and Cleopatra*, 1607

VIVIEN LEIGH AS CLEOPATRA IN SHAKESPEARE'S 'ANTONY AND CLEOPATRA'

THE PASSIONATE SHEPHERD TO
HIS LOVE

COME live with me and be my Love,
And we will all the pleasures prove
That valleys, groves, hills, and fields,
Woods or steepy mountain yields.

And we will sit upon the rocks,
Seeing the shepherds feed their flocks
By shallow rivers, to whose falls
Melodious birds sing madrigals.

And I will make thee beds of roses
And a thousand fragrant posies;
A cap of flowers, and a kirtle
Embroidered all with leaves of myrtle;

A gown made of the finest wool
Which from our pretty lambs we pull;
Fair linëd slippers for the cold,
With buckles of the purest gold;

A belt of straw and ivy-buds
With coral clasps and amber studs;
And if these pleasures may thee move,
Come live with me and be my Love . . .

CHRISTOPHER MARLOWE
in *England's Helicon*, 1600

IT WAS A BEAUTY THAT I SAW

It was a beauty that I saw
    So pure, so perfect, as the frame
    Of all the universe was lame,
To that one figure, could I draw,
Or give least line of it a law!

A skein of silk without a knot,
    A fair march made without a halt,
    A curious form without a fault,
A printed book without a blot,
All beauty, and without a spot!

BEN JONSON, *The New Inn*, 1631

In her sight there was Elysium; her smile was heaven; her voice was enchantment; the air of love waved round her, breathing balm into my heart: for a little while I had sat with the gods at their golden tables, I had tasted of all earth's bliss.

WILLIAM HAZLITT, *Liber Amoris*, 1823

BEAUTY'S EXCELLENCY

GAZE not on swans, in whose soft breast
A full-hatched beauty seems to nest;
Nor snow, which falling from the sky
Hovers in its virginity.

Gaze not on roses, though new blown,
Graced with a fresh complexïon;
Nor lilies, which no subtle bee
Hath robbed by kissing chymistry.

Gaze not on that pure milky way,
Where night vies splendour with the day;
Nor pearl, whose silver walls confine
The riches of an Indian mine.

For if my Emperess appears,
Swans moulting die, snow melts to tears,
Roses do blush and hang their heads,
Pale lilies shrink into their beds:

The milky way rides post to shroud
Its baffled glory in a cloud;
And pearls do climb into her ear,
To hang themselves for envy there . . .

HENRY NOEL
H. Lawes' *Airs and Dialogues*, 1653

LOVE'S PURSUIT

TURN I my looks unto the skies,
Love with his arrows wounds mine eyes:
If so I gaze upon the ground,
Love then in every flower is found:
Search I the shade to fly my pain,
He meets me in the shade again:
Wend I to walk in secret grove,
Ev'n there I melt with sacred Love:
If so I bain me in the spring,
Ev'n on the brink I hear him sing:
If so I meditate alone,
He will be partner of my moan:
If so I mourn, he weeps with me,
And where I am, there will he be.
When as I talk of Rosalind,
The god from coyness waxeth kind,
And seems in selfsame flames to fry,
Because he loves as well as I;
Sweet Rosalind, for pity, rue!
For why than love I am more true:
He, if he speed, will quickly fly;
But in thy love I live and die.

THOMAS LODGE
Rosalind, 1590

A LOVE-SICK COURTIER

MINIATURE BY NICHOLAS HILLIARD *c.* 1590

THE NEPTUNE DISH : ROMAN SILVER FROM THE MILDENHALL TREASURE : FOURTH CENTURY

THE SEASON MADE FOR JOYS

YOUTH's the season made for joys,
    Love is then our duty:
She alone who that employs
    Well deserves her beauty.
        Let's be gay
        While we may:
Beauty's a flower despised in decay.

Let us drink and sport today,
    Ours is not tomorrow.
Love with youth flies swift away:
    Age is nought but sorrow.
        Dance and sing
        Time's on the wing:
Life never knows the return of Spring.

JOHN GAY
The Beggar's Opera, 1728

LOVE IN ARCADY

So it is, Mistress, said he, that yesterday driving my sheep up to the stately hill which lifts his head over the fair city of Mantinea, I happened upon the side of it, in a little falling of the ground which was a rampier against the sun's rage, to perceive a young maid, truly of the finest stamp of beauty, and that which made her beauty the more admirable, there was at all no art added to the helping of it. For her apparel was but such as shepherds' daughters are wont to wear: and as for her hair, it hung down at the free liberty of its goodly length, but that sometimes falling before the clear stars of her sight, she was forced to put it behind her ears, and so open again the treasure of her perfections, which that for a while had in part hidden. In her lap there lay a shepherd, so wrapped up in that well-liked place that I could discern no piece of his face; but as mine eyes were attent in that, her angel-like voice strake mine ears with this song:

My true love hath my heart, and I have his,
By just exchange, one for the other given,
I hold his dear, and mine he cannot miss:
There never was a better bargain driven.

His heart in me, keeps me and him in one,
My heart in him, his thoughts and senses guides:
He loves my heart, for once it was his own:
I cherish his, because in me it bides. . .

SIR PHILIP SIDNEY
The Countess of Pembroke's Arcadia, 1598

AN UNDYING STORY

ONLY a man harrowing clods
　　In a slow silent walk
With an old horse that stumbles and nods
　　Half asleep as they stalk.

Only thin smoke without flame
　　From the heaps of couch-grass;
Yet this will go onward the same
　　Though Dynasties pass.

Yonder a maid and her wight
　　Come whispering by:
War's annals will cloud into night
　　Ere their story die.

THOMAS HARDY, 'In Time of the Breaking
of Nations', *Poems of War and Patriotism*, 1915

Lie still my Dear, why dost thou rise?

The light that shines, comes from thine eyes;

The day breaks not, it is my heart, To think that

WORDS AND MUSIC ANONYMOUS, c. 1612

thou and I   must part.   oh!— stay,   oh!—

stay,   oh! stay, or else   my joys — must die, and per =

ish in their in — — — fan cy.

MUSIC TRANSCRIBED AND EDITED BY ARNOLD DOLMETSCH

TIME TAKES WING

Time is a feathered thing,
  And, whilst I praise
The sparklings of thy looks and call them rays,
    Takes wing,
  Leaving behind him as he flies
An unperceivëd dimness in thine eyes.
  His minutes, whilst they're told,
    Do make us old;
  And every sand of his fleet glass,
  Increasing age as it doth pass,
  Insensibly sows wrinkles there
  Where flowers and roses do appear.
  Whilst we do speak, our fire
  Doth into ice expire,
    Flames turn to frost;
    And ere we can
  Know how our crow turns swan,
  Or how a silver snow
  Springs there where jet did grow,
Our fading spring is in dull winter lost.

Since, then, the Night hath hurled
    Darkness, love's shade,
  Over its enemy the Day, and made
    The world
  Just such a blind and shapeless thing
As 'twas before light did from darkness spring,
  Let us employ its treasure
  And make shade pleasure:

Let's number out the hours by blisses,
And count the minutes by our kisses;
    Let the heavens new motions feel
    And by our embraces wheel;
    And, whilst we try the way
    By which Love doth convey
        Soul unto soul,
        And mingling so
Makes them such raptures know
As makes them entrancëd lie
    In mutual ecstasy,
Let the harmonious spheres in music roll!

JASPER MAYNE, *The Amorous War*, 1648

Now let us sport us while we may,
And now, like amorous birds of prey,
Rather at once our time devour,
Than languish in his slow-chapt power.
Let us roll all our strength and all
Our sweetness up into one ball,
And tear our pleasures, with rough strife,
Thorough the iron gates of life;
Thus, though we cannot make our sun
Stand still, yet we will make him run.

ANDREW MARVELL, from 'To his Coy Mistress',
Miscellaneous Poems, 1681 (written before 1653)

77

BEAUTY, TO ARMS!

And now, unveiled, the toilet stands displayed,
Each silver vase in mystic order laid.
First, robed in white, the Nymph intent adores,
With head uncovered, the cosmetic powers.
A heavenly image in the glass appears,
To that she bends, to that her eyes she rears;
Th' inferior Priestess, at her altar's side,
Trembling, begins the sacred rites of pride.
Unnumbered treasures ope at once, and here
The various offerings of the world appear;
From each she nicely culls with curious toil,
And decks the Goddess with the glittering spoil.
This casket India's glowing gems unlocks,
And all Arabia breathes from yonder box.
The Tortoise here and Elephant unite,
Transformed to combs, the speckled, and the white.
Here files of pins extend their shining rows,
Puffs, powders, patches, bibles, billet-doux.
Now awful Beauty puts on all its arms;
The fair each moment rises in her charms,
Repairs her smiles, awakens every grace,
And calls forth all the wonders of her face;
Sees by degrees a purer blush arise,
And keener lightnings quicken in her eyes.

ALEXANDER POPE, *The Rape of the Lock,* 1714

QUEEN ANNE WALNUT TOILET MIRROR

ROSA MUNDI : WATER–COLOUR DRAWING BY GEORG EHRET *c.* 1745

THE MESSAGE OF THE ROSE

Go, lovely Rose,
Tell her that wastes her time and me,
That now she knows,
When I resemble her to thee,
How sweet and fair she seems to be.

Tell her that's young,
And shuns to have her graces spied,
That hadst thou sprung
In deserts where no men abide,
Thou must have uncommended died.

Small is the worth
Of beauty from the light retired:
Bid her come forth,
Suffer herself to be desired,
And not blush so to be admired.

Then die—that she
The common fate of all things rare
May read in thee;
How small a part of time they share
That are so wondrous sweet and fair!

EDMUND WALLER, *Poems, &c.,* 1645

WHITHER SO FAST?

WHITHER so fast? See how the kindly flowers
  Perfume the air, and all to make thee stay.
The climbing woodbind, clipping all these bowers,
  Clips thee likewise for fear thou pass away.
  Fortune, our friend, our foe will not gainsay.
Stay but awhile, Phoebe no tell-tale is:
She her Endymion, I'll my Phoebe kiss.

Fear not, the ground seeks but to kiss thy feet.
  Hark, hark how Philomela sweetly sings,
Whilst water-wanton fishes, as they meet,
  Strike crotchet time amidst these crystal springs,
  And Zephyrus 'mongst the leaves sweet murmur rings.
Stay but awhile, Phoebe no tell-tale is;
She her Endymion, I'll my Phoebe kiss.

See how the heliotrope, herb of the sun,
  Though he himself long since be gone to bed,
Is not of force thine eyes' bright beams to shun,
  But with their warmth his goldy leaves unspread,
  And on my knee invites thee rest thy head.
Stay but awhile, Phoebe no tell-tale is;
She her Endymion, I'll my Phoebe kiss.

ANONYMOUS, in F. Pilkington's
Songs or Airs, 1605

LOVE'S BAIT

On yon fair brook's enamelled side
  Behold my Chloe stands!
Her angle trembles o'er the tide,
  As conscious of her hands.

Calm as the gentle waves appear
  Her thoughts serenely flow,
Calm as the softly breathing air
  That curls the brook below.

Such charms her sparkling eyes disclose,
  With such soft power endued,
She seems a new-born Venus 'rose
  From the transparent flood.

From each green bank and mossy cave
  The scaly race repair;
They sport beneath the crystal wave,
  And kiss her image there.

Here the bright silver eel enrolled
  In shining volumes lies,
There basks the carp bedroopt with gold
  In the sunshine of her eyes.

With hungry pikes in wanton play
　　The timorous trouts appear;
The hungry pikes forget to prey,
　　The timorous trouts to fear.

With equal haste the thoughtless crew
　　To the fair tempter fly;
Nor grieve they, whilst her eyes they view,
　　That by her hand they die.

Thus I too viewed the nymph of late;
　　Ah! simple fish, beware!
Soon will you find my wretched fate,
　　And struggle in the snare.

But, fair-one, though these toils succeed,
　　Of conquest be not vain;
Nor think o'er all the scaly breed
　　Unpunished thus to reign.

Remember, in a watery glass
　　His charms Narcissus spied,
When for his own bewitching face
　　The youth despaired, and died.

No more, then, harmless fish ensnare,
　　No more such wiles pursue,
Lest, whilst you baits for them prepare,
　　Love finds out one for you.

SOAME JENYNS, *Poems*, 1752

LADY CAROLINE LEIGH, ANGLING : PAINTING BY ARTHUR DEVIS *c.* 1744

UNDINE : DRAWING BY FRANCOIS BOUCHER *c.* 1753

SEA-BORN BEAUTY

FROM out of water n'er
Did rise a shape so fair;
Nor could it e'er to sight
Reflect a form so bright.
Such sweetness, nor such grace,
Shined not in Venus' face,
When froth did it enclose
As 'bove the waves it rose,
And in white circles crowned
The whiter goddess round.
Less pleasing she did shew
Her naked glories new,
Though all the deep then smiled
To see the sea-born child.

No undisturbèd brook
In which the heavens choose to look
Sees such a beauty move
As this reflects above.
No deeps such treasures know
As what this hides below.

RICHARD LEIGH, *Poems*, 1675

THE GAMESTER

When first my youthful, sinful age
   Grew master of my ways,
Appointing error for my page
   And darkness for my days,
I flung away, and with full cry
   Of wild affections rid
In post for pleasures, bent to try
   All gamesters that would bid.
I played with fire, did counsel spurn,
   Made life my common stake;
But never thought that fire would burn,
   Or that a soul could ache.

HENRY VAUGHAN
from 'The Garland', *Silex Scintillans*
Part II, 1655

THE SUFFERING HEART

No, no, poor suffering heart, no change endeavour;
Choose to sustain the smart, rather than leave her.
My ravished eyes behold such charms about her.
I can die with her, but not live without her.
One tender sigh of hers, to see me languish,
Will more than pay the price of my past anguish.
Beware, O cruel fair, how you smile on me,
'Twas a kind look of yours that has undone me.

Love has in store for me one happy minute,
And she will end my pain who did begin it;
Then, no day void of bliss or pleasure leaving,
Ages shall slide away without perceiving:
Cupid shall guard the door, the more to please us,
And keep out Time and Death, when they would seize us:
Time and Death shall depart, and say, in flying,
Love has found out a way to live by dying.

JOHN DRYDEN, *Cleomenes*, 1692

TO HIS WATCH

UNCESSANT minutes, whilst you move you tell
   The time that tells our life, which though it run
Never so fast or far, your new-begun
   Short steps shall overtake; for though life well

May 'scape his own account, it shall not yours:
   You are Death's auditors, that both divide
And sum whate'er that life inspired endures
   Past a beginning, and through you we bide

The doom of Fate, whose unrecalled decree
   You date, bring, execute; making what's new
(Ill and good) old; for as we die in you,
   You die in Time, Time in Eternity.

EDWARD HERBERT,
BARON HERBERT OF CHERBURY
Occasional Verses, 1665 (written before 1648)

WATCH IN BRASS CASE : BY SIMON BARTRAM *c.* 1640

THE LADY SOPHIA PELHAM : PAINTING BY SIR FRANCIS GRANT 1853

THE LAST RIDE TOGETHER

I SAID—Then, dearest, since 'tis so,
Since now at length my fate I know,
Since nothing all my love avails,
Since all my life seemed meant for fails,
   Since this was written and needs must be—
My whole heart rises up to bless
Your name in pride and thankfulness!
Take back the hope you gave—I claim
Only a memory of the same,
—And this beside, if you will not blame;
   Your leave for one more last ride with me

My mistress bent that brow of hers,
Those deep dark eyes where pride demurs
When pity would be softening through,
Fixed me a breathing-while or two
   With life or death in the balance—Right!
The blood replenished me again;
My last thought was at least not vain:
I and my mistress, side by side
Shall be together, breathe and ride,
So, one day more am I deified.
   Who knows but the world may end to-night?

Hush! if you saw some western cloud
All billowy-bosomed, over-bowed
By many benedictions—sun's
And moon's and evening-star's at once—
   And so, you, looking and loving best,
Conscious grew, your passion drew

Cloud, sunset, moonrise, star-shine too,
Down on you, near and yet more near,
Till flesh must fade for heaven was here!—
Thus leant she and linger'd—joy and fear!
    Thus lay she a moment on my breast.

Then we began to ride. My soul
Smoothed itself out, a long-cramped scroll
Freshening and fluttering in the wind.
Past hopes already lay behind.
    What need to strive with a life awry?
Had I said that, had I done this,
So might I gain, so might I miss.
Might she have loved me? just as well
She might have hated, who can tell!
Where had I been now if the worst befell?
    And here we are riding, she and I . . .

What does it all mean, poet? Well,
Your brains beat into rhythm, you tell
What we felt only; you expressed
You hold things beautiful the best,
    And pace them in rhyme so, side by side.
'Tis something, nay 'tis much: but then,
Have you yourself what's best for men?
Are you, poor, sick, old ere your time—
Nearer one whit your own sublime
Than we who never have turned a rhyme?
    Sing, riding's a joy! For me, I ride.

ROBERT BROWNING, from 'The Last
Ride Together', *Men and Women*, 1855

94

TICHBORNE'S ELEGY

(written in the Tower before his execution)

My prime of youth is but a frost of cares;
   My feast of joy is but a dish of pain;
My crop of corn is but a field of tares;
   And all my good is but vain hope of gain;
The day is past, and yet I saw no sun;
And now I live, and now my life is done.

My tale was heard, and yet it was not told;
   My fruit is fall'n, and yet my leaves are green,
My youth is spent, and yet I am not old;
   I saw the world, and yet I was not seen:
My thread is cut, and yet it is not spun;
And now I live, and now my life is done.

I sought my death, and found it in my womb;
   I looked for life, and saw it was a shade;
I trod the earth, and knew it was my tomb;
   And now I die, and now I was but made;
My glass is full, and now my glass is run;
And now I live, and now my life is done.

CHIDIOCK TICHBORNE
Verses of Praise and Joy, 1586

AT THE CLOSE OF SPRING

THE garlands fade that Spring so lately wove,
    Each simple flower which she had nursed in dew,
Anemones that spangled every grove,
    The primrose wan, and hare-bell mildly blue.
No more shall violets linger in the dell,
    Or purple orchis variegate the plain,
Till Spring again shall call forth every bell,
    And dress with humid hands her wreaths again.
Ah! poor humanity! so frail, so fair,
    Are the fond visions of thy early day,
Till tyrant passion and corrosive care
    Bid all thy fairy colours fade away!
Another May new buds and flowers shall bring;
Ah! why has happiness no second Spring?

CHARLOTTE SMITH, Elegiac Sonnets, 1800

SWEET DAY

SWEET day, so cool, so calm, so bright!
   The bridal of the earth and sky—
The dew shall weep thy fall to-night;
   For thou must die.

Sweet rose, whose hue angry and brave
   Bids the rash gazer wipe his eye,
Thy root is ever in its grave,
   And thou must die.

Sweet spring, full of sweet days and roses,
   A box where sweets compacted lie,
My music shows ye have your closes,
   And all must die.

Only a sweet and virtuous soul,
   Like seasoned timber, never gives;
But though the whole world turn to coal,
   Then chiefly lives.

GEORGE HERBERT, *The Temple*, 1633

SEE WHERE MY LOVE SITS

FAIR is my Love that feeds among the lilies,
The lilies growing in that pleasant garden
Where Cupid's Mount that well belovèd hill is,
And where that little god himself is warden.
See where my Love sits in the beds of spices,
Beset all round with camphor, myrrh, and roses,
And interlaced with curious devices
Which her apart from all the world incloses!
There doth she tune her lute for her delight,
And with sweet music makes the ground to move,
Whilst I, poor I, do sit in heavy plight,
Wailing alone my unrespected love:
   Not daring rush into so rare a place,
   That gives to her, and she to it, a grace.

BARTHOLOMEW GRIFFIN
Fidessa, 1596

THE TIDES OF LOVE

Look how the pale queen of the silent night
Doth cause the ocean to attend upon her,
And he, as long as she is in his sight,
With his full tide is ready her to honour:
But when the silver wagon of the moon
Is mounted up so high he cannot follow,
The sea calls home his crystal waves to moan,
And with low ebb doth manifest his sorrow.
So you, that are the sovereign of my heart,
Have all my joys attending on your will:
My joys low ebbing when you do depart,
When you return, their tide my heart doth fill.
  So as you come, and as you do depart,
  Joys ebb and flow within my tender heart.

CHARLES BEST, in
A Poetical Rhapsody, 1602

BEAUTY'S SELF

My Love in her attire doth show her wit,
    It doth so well become her;
For every season she hath dressings fit,
    For Winter, Spring and Summer.
No beauty she doth miss
    When all her robes are on:
But Beauty's self she is
    When all her robes are gone.

ANONYMOUS, in
A Poetical Rhapsody, 1602

THE TOILET OF VENUS : PAINTING BY PHILIP WILSON STEER 1898

THE KISS : SCULPTURE IN MARBLE BY AUGUSTE RODIN 1886

THE KISS

THE moth's kiss, first!
Kiss me as if you made believe
You were not sure, this eve,
How my face, your flower, had pursed
Its petals up; so, here and there
You brush it, till I grow aware
Who wants me, and wide open burst.

The bee's kiss, now!
Kiss me as if you entered gay
My heart at some noonday,
A bud that dares not disallow
The claim, so all is rendered up,
And passively its shattered cup
Over your head to sleep I bow.

ROBERT BROWNING, from
'In a Gondola', *Dramatic Lyrics*, 1842

A BIRTHDAY

My heart is like a singing bird
   Whose nest is in a watered shoot;
My heart is like an apple-tree
   Whose boughs are bent with thick-set fruits;
My heart is like a rainbow shell
   That paddles in a halcyon sea;
My heart is gladder than all these,
   Because my love is come to me.

Raise me a daïs of silk and down;
   Hang it with vair and purple dyes;
Carve it in doves and pomegranates,
   And peacocks with a hundred eyes;
Work it in gold and silver grapes,
   In leaves and silver fleurs-de-lys;
Because the birthday of my life
   Is come, my love is come to me.

CHRISTINA GEORGINA ROSSETTI
Goblin Market and other Poems, 1862

THE GOOD-MORROW

I WONDER, by my troth, what thou and I
Did, till we loved? were we not weaned till then?
But sucked on country pleasures, childishly?
Or snorted we in the Seven Sleepers' den?
'Twas so; but this, all pleasures fancies be;
If ever any beauty I did see,
Which I desired, and got, 'twas but a dream of thee.

And now good-morrow to our waking souls,
Which watch not one another out of fear;
For love all love of other sights controls,
And makes one little room an everywhere.
Let sea-discoverers to new worlds have gone;
Let maps to other, worlds on worlds have shown;
Let us possess one world; each hath one, and is one.

My face in thine eye, thine in mine appears,
And true plain hearts do in the faces rest;
Where can we find two better hemispheres
Without sharp north, without declining west;
Whatever dies, was not mixed equally;
If our two loves be one, or thou and I
Love so alike that none can slacken, none can die.

JOHN DONNE
Poems, 1633 (written *c.* 1600)

CONSTANCY

I WENT out at the Eastern Gate,
   I saw the girls in clouds,
Like clouds they were, and soft and bright,
   But in the crowds
I thought on the maid who is my light,
Down-drooping, soft as the grey twilight;
   She is my mate.

I went out by the Tower on the Wall,
   I saw the girls in flower,
Like flowering rushes they swayed and bent,
   But in that hour
I thought on the maid who is my saint,
In her thin white robe and her colouring faint;
   She is my all.

Chinese Lyric, 680 B.C.
translated by HELEN WADDELL

A SPIRIT OF THE WAVES : CHINESE PAINTING AFTER CHI'EN HSÜAN

ARNOLFINI AND HIS BRIDE : PAINTING BY JAN VAN EYCK 1434

A SEAL UPON THINE HEART

SET me as a seal upon thine heart, as a seal upon thine arm; for love is strong as death; jealousy is cruel as the grave; the coals thereof are coals of fire, which hath a most vehement flame. Many waters cannot quench love, neither can the floods drown it.

Solomon's Song, viii, 6–7

THE lowest trees have tops; the ant her gall;
    The fly her spleen; the little sparks their heat;
The slender hairs cast shadows, though but small;
    And bees have stings, although they be not great.
Seas have their source, and so have shallow springs:
And love is love, in beggars as in kings.

Where rivers smoothest run, deep are the fords;
    The dial stirs, yet none perceives it move;
The firmest faith is in the fewest words;
    The turtles cannot sing, and yet they love.
True hearts have eyes and ears, no tongues to speak;
They hear and see and sigh; and then they break.

SIR EDWARD DYER, in
A Poetical Rhapsody, 1602

SUMMER NIGHT

Now sleeps the crimson petal, now the white;
Nor waves the cypress in the palace walk;
Nor winks the gold fin in the porphyry font:
The firefly wakens: waken thou with me.

Now droops the milk-white peacock like a ghost,
And like a ghost she glimmers on to me.

Now lies the Earth all Danaë to the stars,
And all thy heart lies open unto me.

Now slides the silent meteor on, and leaves
A shining furrow, as thy thoughts in me.

Now folds the lily all her sweetness up,
And slips into the bosom of the lake:
So fold thyself, my dearest, thou, and slip
Into my bosom and be lost in me.

ALFRED, BARON TENNYSON
The Princess, 1847

A HEART AT REST

Not, Celia, that I juster am
   Or better than the rest;
For I would change each hour, like them,
   Were not my heart at rest.

But I am tied to very thee
   By every thought I have;
Thy face I only care to see,
   Thy heart I only crave.

All that in woman is adored
   In thy dear self I find;
For the whole sex can but afford
   The handsome and the kind.

Why then should I seek further store,
   And still make love anew?
When change itself can give no more,
   'Tis easy to be true.

SIR CHARLES SEDLEY
Miscellaneous Works, 1702 (written *c.* 1670)

LULLABY

UPON my lap my sovereign sits
  And sucks upon my breast.
Meanwhile his love sustains my life,
  And gives my body rest.
      Sing lullaby, my little boy,
      Sing lullaby, my only joy.

When thou hast taken thy repast,
  Repose, my babe, on me;
So may thy mother and thy nurse
  Thy cradle also be.
      Sing lullaby, my little boy,
      Sing lullaby, my only joy.

I grieve that duty doth not work
  All what my wishing would,
Because I would not be to thee
  But in the best I should.
      Sing lullaby, my little boy,
      Sing lullaby, my only joy.

Yet as I am, and as I may,
  I must and will be thine,
Though all too little for thyself,
  Vouchsafing to be mine.
      Sing lullaby, my little boy,
      Sing lullaby, my only joy.

RICHARD VERSTEGAN, *Odes*, 1601

MADONNA AND CHILD : SCULPTURE IN STONE BY HENRY MOORE 1943

GRACE

WHAT though no grants of royal donors
   With pompous titles grace our blood?
We'll shine in more substantial honours,
   And, to be noble, we'll be good.

Our name, while virtue thus we tender,
   Will sweetly sound where-e'er 'tis spoke:
And all the great ones, they shall wonder
   How they respect such little folk . . .

Through youth and age, in love excelling,
   We'll hand in hand together tread;
Sweet-smiling peace shall crown our dwelling,
   And babes, sweet-smiling babes, our bed.

How should I love the pretty creatures,
   While round my knees they fondly clung,
To see them look their mother's features,
   To hear them lisp their mother's tongue!

And, when with envy Time transported
   Shall think to rob us of our joys,
You'll, in your girls, again be courted,
   And I'll go wooing in my boys.

ANONYMOUS, *Miscellaneous Poems*
by Several Hands, 1726

SOFT SEPTEMBER

NOT every man has gentians in his house
in Soft September, at slow, Sad Michaelmas.

Bavarian gentians, big and dark, only dark
darkening the day-time torch-like with the smoking blueness of
    Pluto's gloom,
ribbed and torch-like, with their blaze of darkness spread blue
down flattening into points, flattened under the sweep of white day
torch-flower of the blue-smoking darkness, Pluto's dark-blue daze,
black lamps from the halls of Dis, burning dark blue,
giving off darkness, blue darkness, as Demeter's pale lamps give off
    light,
lead me then, lead me the way.

Reach me a gentian, give me a torch
let me guide myself with the blue, forked torch of this flower
down the darker and darker stairs, where blue is darkened on blue-
    ness,
even where Persephone goes, just now, from the frosted September
to the sightless realm where darkness is awake upon the dark
and Persephone herself is but a voice
or a darkness invisible enfolded in the deeper dark
of the arms Plutonic, and pierced with the passion of dense gloom,
among the splendour of torches of darkness, shedding darkness on
    the lost bride and her groom.

D. H. LAWRENCE
'Bavarian Gentians', in Last Poems, 1933

THE FALL OF THE LEAF

In the beginning of the world we presume all things to have been
produced in their best state; all was perfect, and yet how soon a
decay! All was summer, and yet how soon a fall of the leaf!

JOHN DONNE

It was my thirtieth year to heaven
Woke to my hearing from harbour and neighbour wood
  And the mussel pooled and the heron
        Priested shore
     The morning beckon
With water praying and call of seagull and rook
And the knock of sailing boats on the net webbed wall
  Myself to set foot
     That second
In the still sleeping town and set forth.

My birthday began with the water—
Birds and the birds of the winged trees flying my name
  Above the farms and the white horses
     And I rose
    In rainy autumn
And walked abroad in a shower of all my days.
High tide and the heron dived when I took the road
  Over the border
    And the gates
Of the town closed as the town awoke.

A springful of larks in a rolling
Cloud and the roadside bushes brimming with whistling
    Blackbirds and the sun of October
                Summery
            On the hill's shoulder,
Here were fond climates and sweet singers suddenly
Come in the morning where I wandered and listened
        To the rain wringing
            Wind blow cold
    In the wood faraway under me.

    Pale rain over the dwindling harbour
And over the sea wet church the size of a snail
    With its horns through mist and the castle
                Brown as owls
            But all the gardens
Of spring and summer were blooming in the tall tales
Beyond the border and under the lark full cloud.
        There could I marvel
            My birthday
    Away but the weather turned around.

    It turned away from the blithe country
And down the other air and the blue altered sky
    Streamed again a wonder of summer
                With apples
            Pears and red currants
And I saw in the turning so clearly a child's
Forgotten mornings when he walked with his mother
        Through the parables
            Of sunlight
    And the legends of the green chapels.

And the twice told fields of infancy
That his tears burned my cheeks and his heart moved in mine.
    These were the woods the river and sea
         Where a boy
      In the listening
Summertime of the dead whispered the truth of his joy
To the trees and the stones and the fish in the tide.
      And the mystery
        Sang alive
Still in the water and singingbirds.

    And there could I marvel my birthday
Away but the weather turned around. And the true
    Joy of the long dead child sang burning
        In the sun.
      It was my thirtieth
Year to heaven stood there then in the summer noon
Though the town below lay leaved with October blood.
      O may my heart's truth
        Still be sung
On this high hill in a year's turning.

DYLAN THOMAS, *Deaths and Entrances*, 1946

AUTUMN SUNSET

THE sun sets on some retired meadow, where no house is visible, with all the glory and splendour that it lavishes on cities, and, perchance, as it has never set before—where there is but a solitary marsh-hawk to have his wings gilded by it, or only a musquash looks out from his cabin, and there is some little black-veined brook in the midst of the marsh, just beginning to meander, winding slowly round a decaying stump. We walked in so pure and bright a light, gilding the withered grass and leaves, so softly and serenely bright, I thought I had never bathed in such a golden flood, without a ripple or a murmur to it. The west side of every wood and rising ground gleamed like the boundary of Elysium, and the sun on our backs seemed like a gentle herdsman driving us home at evening.

So we saunter toward the Holy Land, till one day the sun shall shine more brightly than ever he has done, shall perchance shine into our minds and hearts, and light up our whole lives with a great awakening light, as warm and serene and golden as on a bankside in autumn.

HENRY DAVID THOREAU
from 'Walking',
The Atlantic Monthly, 1862

NOVEMBER SKIES

THAN these November skies
Is no sky lovelier. The clouds are deep;
Into their grey the subtle spies
Of colour creep,
Changing that high austerity to delight,
Till even the leaden interfolds are bright.
And, where the cloud breaks, faint far azure peers
Ere a thin flushing cloud again
Shuts up that loveliness, or shares.
The huge great clouds move slowly, gently, as
Reluctant the quick sun should shine in vain,
Holding in bright caprice their rain.
    And when of colours none,
Nor rose, nor amber, nor the scarce late green
Is truly seen,—
In all the myriad grey,
In silver height and dusky deep, remain
The loveliest,
Faint purple flushes of the unvanquished sun.

JOHN FREEMAN, *Stone Trees*, 1916

WINTER EVENING

Now stir the fire, and close the shutters fast,
Let fall the curtains, wheel the sofa round,
And, while the bubbling and loud-hissing urn
Throws up a steamy column, and the cups,
That cheer but not inebriate, wait on each,
So let us welcome peaceful evening in . . .

Oh Winter, ruler of th'inverted year, . . .
I love thee, all unlovely as thou seem'st,
And dreaded as thou art. Thou hold'st the sun
A prisoner in the yet undawning east,
Shortening his journey between morn and noon,
And hurrying him, impatient of his stay,
Down to the rosy west; but kindly still
Compensating his loss with added hours
Of social converse and instructive ease,
And gathering, at short notice, in one group
The family dispersed, and fixing thought,
Not less dispersed by day-light and its cares.
I crown thee king of intimate delights,
Fire-side enjoyments, home-born happiness,
And all the comforts that the lowly roof
Of undisturbed retirement and the hours
Of long uninterrupted evening know.

WILLIAM COWPER, *The Task,* 1785

THE TEA-PARTY : STAFFORDSHIRE POTTERY GROUP *c.* 1745

MARGOT FONTEYN IN 'LES SYLPHIDES'

WHERE WERE THE WHITE FLOWERS?

LIFE in a day: he took his girl to the ballet;
Being shortsighted himself could hardly see it—
    The white skirts in the grey
    Glade and the swell of the music
    Lifting the white sails.

Calyx upon calyx, canterbury bells in the breeze
The flowers on the left mirror to the flowers on the right
    And the naked arms above
    The powdered faces moving
    Like seaweed in a pool.

Now, he thought, we are floating—ageless, oarless—
Now there is no separation, from now on
    You will be wearing white
    Satin and a red sash
    Under the waltzing trees.

But the music stopped, the dancers took their curtain,
The river had come to a lock—a shuffle of programmes—
    And we cannot continue down
    Stream unless we are ready
    To enter the lock and drop.

So they were married—to be the more together—
And found they were never again so much together,
    Divided by the morning tea,
    By the evening paper,
    By children and tradesmen's bills.

Waking at times in the night she found assurance
In his regular breathing but wondered whether
    It was really worth it and where
    The river had flowed away
And where were the white flowers.

LOUIS MACNEICE, 'Les Sylphides', in
Plant and Phantom, 1941

LOST CONTENT

Into my heart an air that kills
    From yon far country blows:
What are those blue remembered hills,
    What spires, what farms are those?

That is the land of lost content,
    I see it shining plain,
The happy highways where I went
    And cannot come again.

A. E. HOUSMAN
A Shropshire Lad, 1896

NOUS N'IRONS PLUS AU BOIS

Nous n'irons plus au bois, les lauriers sont coupés.
Les Amours des bassins, les Naïades en groupe
Voient reluire au soleil en cristaux découpés
Les flots silencieux qui coulaient de leur coupe.
Les lauriers sont coupés, et le cerf aux abois
Tressaile au son du cor; nous n'irons plus au bois,
Où des enfants charmants riait la folle troupe
Sous les regards des lys aux pleurs du ciel trempés.
Voici l'herbe qu'on fauche et les lauriers qu'on coupe.
Nous n'irons plus au bois, les lauriers sont coupés.

THÉODORE DE BANVILLE,
Poésies Nouvelles, 1890

MATURITY

ALL love at first, like generous wine,
Ferments and frets, until 'tis fine;
But when 'tis settled on the lee,
And from the impurer matter free,
Becomes the richer still, the older,
And proves the pleasanter, the colder.

SAMUEL BUTLER, *Genuine Remains*, 1759
(written in seventeenth century)

127

THE FEET IN THE FOREST

WILL they ever come to me, ever again,
   The long long dances
On through the dark till the dim stars wane?
    Shall I feel the dew on my throat, and the stream
    Of wind in my hair? Shall our white feet gleam
      In the dim expanses?
Oh, feet of a fawn to the greenwood fled,
   Alone in the grass and the loveliness;
Leap of the hunted, no more in dread,
   Beyond the snares and the deadly press:
Yet a voice and a fear and a haste of hounds;
   A wildly labouring, fiercely fleet,
Onward yet by river and glen.
   Is it joy or terror, ye storm-swift feet?
To the dear lone lands untroubled of men,
Where no voice sounds, and amid the shadowy green
The little things of the woodland live unseen.

EURIPIDES, *The Bacchae*, translated
by Gilbert Murray

PRE-HISTORIC CAVE-PAINTING : LASCAUX, FRANCE

TOM OLDAKER ON 'PICKLE' : PAINTING BY BEN MARSHALL 1800

AS DAY FAILS

... But hunters as day fails
Will take the short-cut home across the fields;
With slackened rein will stoop through darkening wealds;
With creaking leathers skirt the swedes and kales;
Patient, adventuring still,
A horse's ears bob on the distant hill;
He starts to hear
A pheasant chuck or whirr, having the fear
In him of ages filled with war and raid,
Night gallop, ambuscade;
Remembering adventures of his kin
With giant winged worms that coiled round mountain bases,
And Nordic tales of young gods riding races
Up courses of the rainbow; here, within
The depth of Hampshire hedges, does he dream
How Athens woke, to hear above her roofs
The welkin flash and thunder to the hoofs
Of Dawn's tremendous team?

DOROTHY WELLESLEY
from 'Horses', *Lost Lane*, 1925

ON THE DEATH OF HIS MISTRESS

Ask me not why the rose doth fade,
    Lilies look pale, and flowers die;
Question not why the myrtle shade
    Her wonted shadows doth deny.

Seek not to know from whence begun
    The sadness of the nightingale,
Nor why the heliotrope and sun
    Their constant amity do fail.

The turtle's grief look not upon,
    Nor why the palm-tree doth mourn,
When widow-like they're left alone,
    Nor phoenix, why her self doth burn.

For she is dead which life did give
    Unto those things that here I name;
They fade, change, wither, cease to live,
    Pine, and consume into a flame.

PATTERICKE JENKYN, *Amorea,* 1661

NO WORST, THERE IS NONE

No worst, there is none. Pitched past pitch of grief,
More pangs will, schooled at forepangs, wilder wring.
Comforter, where, where is your comforting?
Mary, mother of us, where is your relief?
My cries heave, herds-long; huddle in a main, a chief
Woe, world-sorrow; on an age-old anvil wince and sing—
Then lull, then leave off. Fury had shrieked 'No lingering!
Let me be fell: force I must be brief.'

  O the mind, mind has mountains; cliffs of fall
Frightful, sheer, no-man-fathomed. Hold them cheap
May who ne'er hung there. Nor does long our small
Durance deal with that steep or deep. Here! creep,
Wretch, under a comfort serves in a whirlwind: all
Life death does end and each day dies with sleep.

GERARD MANLEY HOPKINS
Poems, 1918 (written *c.* 1886)

TO A DANCING GIRL

Two top-knots not yet plaited into one.
Of thirty years—just beyond half.
You who are really a lady of silks and satins
Are now become my hill and stream companion!
At the spring fountains together we splash and play:
On the lovely trees together we climb and sport.
Her cheeks grow rosy, as she quickens her sleeve-dancing:
Her brows grow sad, as she slows her song's tune.
Don't go singing the Song of the Willow Branches,
When there's no one here with a heart for you to break!

PO CHU-I, written *c.* 830
translated by Arthur Waley

*This poem was written when the poet was about sixty-five, and was
addressed to a little dancing girl who had accompanied him to the mountains.
The 'Song of the Willow Branches' was a plaintive love-song written by
Po Chū-i himself.*

CHINESE SLEEVE DANCER : TA'NG POTTERY FIGURE

THE GARDEN OF FELICITY : INDIAN MINIATURE
BY BISHAN DAS AND NANHA c. 1590

MY ARBOUR AND MY TOMB

GIVE me a little plot of ground,
Where might I with the Sun agree;
Though every day he walk the round,
My garden he should seldom see.

Those tulips, that such wealth display
To court my eye, shall lose their name,
Though now they listen, as if they
Expected I should praise their flame.

But I would see my self appear
Within the violet's drooping head,
On which a melancholy tear
The discontented morn hath shed.

Within their buds let roses sleep,
And virgin lilies on their stem,
Till sighs from lovers glide, and creep
Into their leaves to open them.

I'th' centre of my ground compose
Of bays and yew my Summer room,
Which may so oft as I repose,
Present my arbour and my tomb.

JAMES SHIRLEY, from
'The Garden', *Poems*, 1646

THE NOTE OF SADNESS

THE sea is calm to-night,
The tide is full, the moon lies fair
Upon the Straits;—on the French coast the light
Gleams and is gone; the cliffs of England stand,
Glimmering and vast, out in the tranquil bay,
Come to the window, sweet is the night air!
Only, from the long line of spray
Where the ebb meets the moon-blanched sand,
Listen! you hear the grating roar
Of pebbles which the waves suck back, and fling,
At their return, up the high strand,
Begin, and cease, and then again begin,
With tremulous cadence slow, and bring
The eternal note of sadness in.

MATTHEW ARNOLD, from 'Dover Beach',
New Poems, 1867

THE NOTE OF MADNESS

I AM! yet what I am none cares or knows;
   My friends forsake me like a memory lost.
I am the self-consumer of my woes;
   They rise and vanish in oblivious host,
Like shades in love and death's oblivion lost;
And yet I am, and live with shadows tost

Into the nothingness of scorn and noise,
   Into the living sea of waking dreams,
Where there is neither sense of life, nor joys,
   But the vast shipwreck of my life's esteems;
And e'en the dearest—that I loved the best—
Are strange—nay, rather stranger than the rest.

I long for scenes where man has never trod—
   A place where woman never smiled or wept—
There to abide with my Creator, God,
   And sleep as I in childhood sweetly slept,
Untroubling and untroubled where I lie,
The grass below; above, the vaulted sky.

JOHN CLARE, in Martin's *Life of John Clare*,
1865 (written in Northampton County Asylum)

ASH WEDNESDAY

ALTHOUGH I do not hope to turn again
Although I do not hope
Although I do not hope to turn

Wavering between the profit and the loss
In this brief transit where the dreams cross
The dreamcrossed twilight between birth and dying
(Bless me father) though I do not wish to wish these things
From the wide window towards the granite shore
The white sails still fly seaward, seaward flying
Unbroken wings

And the lost heart stiffens and rejoices
In the lost lilac and the lost sea voices
And the weak spirit quickens to rebel
For the bent golden-rod and the lost sea smell
Quickens to recover
The cry of quail and the whirling plover
And the blind eye creates
The empty forms between the ivory gates
And smell renews the salt savour of the sandy earth

This is the time of tension between dying and birth
The place of solitude where three dreams cross
Between blue rocks
But when the voices shaken from the yew-tree drift away
Let the other yew be shaken and reply

Blessëd sister, holy mother, spirit of the fountain, spirit of
    the garden,
Suffer us not to mock ourselves with falsehood
Teach us to care and not to care
Teach us to sit still
Even among these rocks
Our peace in His will
And even among these rocks
Sister, mother
And spirit of the river, spirit of the sea,
Suffer me not to be separated

And let my cry come unto Thee.

T. S. ELIOT
Part VI of *Ash Wednesday*, 1930

HE who binds to himself a joy
Does the wingëd life destroy;
But he who kisses the joy as it flies
Lives in eternity's sun rise.

WILLIAM BLAKE
Rossetti MS., *c.* 1793

AND BEAUTY CAME LIKE THE
SETTING SUN

EVERYONE suddenly burst out singing;
And I was filled with such delight
As prisoned birds must find in freedom,
Winging wildly across the white
Orchards and dark-green fields; on—on—and out of sight.

Everyone's voice was suddenly lifted;
And beauty came like the setting sun:
My heart was shaken with tears; and horror
Drifted away . . . O, but Everyone
Was a bird; and the song was wordless; the singing
    will never be done.

SIEGFRIED SASSOON
'Everyone Sang', *Picture Show*, 1919

SUDDEN LIGHT

I HAVE been here before,
But when or how I cannot tell:
I know the grass beyond the door,
The sweet keen smell,
The sighing sound, the lights around the shore.

You have been mine before,—
How long ago I may not know:
But just when at that swallow's soar
Your neck turned so,
Some veil did fall,—I knew it all of yore.

Then, now,—perchance again!
O round mine eyes your tresses shake!
Shall we not lie as we have lain
Thus for Love's sake,
And sleep, and wake, yet never break the chain?

DANTE GABRIEL ROSSETTI
Poems, 1870

THE FIRE OF LOVE

THE fire of love in youthful blood,
Like what is kindled in brushwood,
   But for a moment burns;
Yet in that moment makes a mighty noise,
It crackles, and to vapour turns,
   And soon itself destroys.

But when crept into agèd veins
It slowly burns, and long remains;
   And, with a sullen heat,
Like fire in logs, it glows, and warms 'em long,
And, though the flame be not so great,
   Yet is the heat as strong.

CHARLES SACKVILLE, EARL OF DORSET
The Amorous Bigot, 1690

144

THE BRADSHAW FAMILY : PAINTING BY JOHN ZOFFANY

SPARSHOLT CHURCH, BERKSHIRE : PHOTOGRAPH BY EDWIN SMITH

THE BELL TOLLS

PERCHANCE he for whom this bell tolls may be so ill as that he knows not it tolls for him. And perchance I may think myself so much better than I am, as that they who are about me, and see my state, may have caused it to toll for me, and I know not that. The Church is catholic, universal, so are all her actions. All that she does belongs to all. When she baptizes a child, that action concerns me; for that child is thereby connected to that head which is my head too, and engraffed into that body, whereof I am a member. And when she buries a man, that action concerns me. . . . As therefore the bell that rings to a sermon calls not upon the preacher only, but upon the congregation to come; so this bell calls us all: but how much more me, who am brought too near the door by this sickness . . . The bell doth toll for him that thinks it doth; and though it intermit again, yet from that minute, that that occasion wrought upon him, he is united to God. Who casts not up his eye to the sun when it rises? but who takes off his eye from a comet when that breaks out? Who bends not his ear to any bell, which upon any occasion rings? but who can remove it from that bell, which is passing a piece of himself out of this world? No man is an island, entire of itself; every man is a piece of the continent, a part of the main; if a clod be washed away by the sea, Europe is the less, as well as if a promontory were, as well as if a manor of thy friends or of thine own were; any man's death diminishes me, because I am involved in mankind. And therefore never send to know for whom the bell tolls. It tolls for thee.

JOHN DONNE
Devotions upon Emergent Occasions, 1624

IN AGE I BUD AGAIN

WHO would have thought my shrivelled heart
Could have recovered greenness? It was gone
    Quite under ground, as flowers depart
To feed their mother-root when they have blown,
        Where they together
        All the hard weather,
Dead to the world, keep house unknown.

    These are thy wonders, Lord of Power,
Killing and quickening, bringing down to hell
    And up to heaven in an hour;
Making a chiming of a passing-bell.
        We say amiss,
        This or that is:
Thy word is all, if we could spell . . .

    And now in age I bud again,
After so many deaths I live and write;
    I once more smell the dew and rain,
And relish versing: O my only Light,
        It cannot be
        That I am he
On whom thy tempests fell all night.

GEORGE HERBERT, from 'The Flower',
The Temple, 1633

SING BRAVELY IN MY HEART

SING bravely in my heart, you patient birds
Who all this weary winter wait for spring;
Sing, till such wonder wakens in my words
As I have known long since, beyond all voicing,—
Strong with the beat of blood, wild on the wing,
Rebellious and rejoicing.

Watch with me, inward solemn influence,
Invisible, intangible, unkenned;
Wind of the darkness that shall bear me hence;
O life within my life, flame within flame,
Who mak'st me one with song that has no end,
And with that stillness whence my spirit came.

SIEGFRIED SASSOON
The Heart's Journey, 1928

THE VIRGIN QUEEN'S LAMENT

WHEN I was fair and young, and favour gracëd me,
Of many was I sought, their mistress for to be:
But I did scorn them all, and answered them therefore,
    'Go, go, go, seek some otherwhere!
        Importune me no more!'

How many weeping eyes I made to pine with woe,
How many sighing hearts, I have no skill to show:
Yet I the prouder grew, and answered them therefore,
    'Go, go, go, seek some otherwhere!
        Importune me no more!'

Then spake fair Venus' son, that proud victorious boy,
And said, 'Fine Dame, since that you be so coy,
I will so pluck your plumes that you shall say no more,
    'Go, go, go, seek some otherwhere!
        Importune me no more!'

When he had spake these words, such change grew in my breast
That neither night nor day, since that, I could take any rest:
Then, lo! I did repent that I had said before,
    'Go, go, go, seek some otherwhere!
        Importune me no more!'

Attributed to QUEEN ELIZABETH I
Bodley MS. Rawl. Poet. 85

QUEEN ELIZABETH I : PAINTING ATTRIBUTED TO NICHOLAS HILLIARD *c.* 1585

PORTRAIT OF AN OLD LADY : PAINTING BY REMBRANDT 1634

WHEN YOU ARE OLD

WHEN you are old and gray and full of sleep
   And nodding by the fire, take down this book,
   And slowly read, and dream of the soft look
Your eyes had once, and of their shadows deep;

How many loved your moments of glad grace,
   And loved your beauty with love false or true;
   But one man loved the pilgrim soul in you,
And loved the sorrows of your changing face.

And bending down beside the glowing bars
   Murmur, a little sadly, how love fled
   And paced upon the mountains overhead,
And hid his face amid a crowd of stars.

                WILLIAM BUTLER YEATS
                The Countess Cathleen, 1892

MR PETULENGRO'S OPINION OF
DEATH

'WHAT is your opinion of death, Mr Petulengro?' said I, as I sat down beside him.

'My opinion of death, brother, is much the same as that in the old song of Pharaoh, which I have heard my grandma sing:

Cana marel o manus chivios ande puv,
Ta rovel pa leste o chavo ta romi.

When a man dies, he is cast into the earth, and his wife and child sorrow over him. If he has neither wife nor child, then his father and mother, I suppose; and if he is quite alone in the world, why, then, he is cast into the earth, and there is an end of the matter.'

'And do you think that is the end of man?'

'There's an end of him, brother, more's the pity.'

'Why do you say so?'

'Life is sweet, brother.'

'Do you think so?'

'Think so! There's night and day, brother, both sweet things; sun, moon, and stars, brother, all sweet things; there's likewise a wind on the heath. Life is very sweet, brother; who would wish to die?'

'I would wish to die—'

'You talk like a Gorgio—which is the same as talking like a fool. Were you a Romany Chal, you would talk wiser. Wish to die, indeed! A Romany Chal would wish to live for ever!'

'In sickness, Jasper?'

'There's the sun and stars, brother.'

'In blindness, Jasper?'

'There's the wind on the heath, brother; if I could only feel that,

I would gladly live for ever. Dosta, we'll now go to the tents and put on the gloves; and I'll try to make you feel what a sweet thing it is to be alive, brother.'

GEORGE BORROW, Lavengro, 1851

FINIS

I STROVE with none, for none was worth my strife.
    Nature I loved, and, next to Nature, Art:
I warmed both hands before the fire of life;
    It sinks, and I am ready to depart.

WALTER SAVAGE LANDOR

DEATH stands above me, whispering low
    I know not what into my ear:
Of his strange language all I know
    Is, there is not a word of fear.

WALTER SAVAGE LANDOR
Last Fruit, 1853

FARE WELL

WHEN I lie where shades of darkness
Shall no more assail mine eyes,
Nor the rain make lamentation
　　When the wind sighs;
How will fare the world whose wonder
Was the very proof of me?
Memory fades, must the remembered
　　Perishing be?

Oh, when this my dust surrenders
Hand, foot, lip, to dust again,
May these loved and loving faces
　　Please other men!
May the rusting harvest hedgerow
Still the Traveller's Joy entwine,
And as happy children gather
　　Posies once mine.

Look thy last on all things lovely,
Every hour. Let no night
Seal thy sense in deathly slumber
　　Till to delight
Thou have paid thy utmost blessing;
Since that all things thou wouldst praise
Beauty took from those who loved them
　　In other days.

WALTER DE LA MARE, *Motley*, 1918

LYDIA DWIGHT, DIED 1673 : SALT-GLAZE STONEWARE FIGURE BY JOHN DWIGHT

CLASSICAL COMPOSITION : PAINTING BY FRANCESCO GUARDI

THE GARLANDS WITHER

As withereth the primrose by the river,
As fadeth summer's sun from gliding fountains,
As vanisheth the light-blown bubble ever,
As melteth snow upon the mossy mountains;
So melts, so vanisheth, so fades, so withers
The rose, the shine, the bubble, and the snow
Of praise, pomp, glory, joy—which short life gathers—
Fair praise, vain pomp, sweet glory, brittle joy.
The withered primrose by the mourning river,
The faded summer's sun from weeping fountains,
The light-blown bubble vanishèd for ever,
The molten snow upon the naked mountains,
    Are emblems that the treasures we up-lay
    Soon wither, vanish, fade, and melt away.

For as the snow, whose lawn did overspread
The ambitious hills, which giant-like did threat
To pierce the heaven with their aspiring head,
Naked and bare doth leave their craggy seat;
Whenas the bubble, which did empty fly
The dalliance of the undiscernèd wind,
On whose calm rolling waves it did rely,
Hath shipwreck made, where it did dalliance find;
And when the sunshine which dissolved the snow,
Coloured the bubble with a pleasant vary,
And made the rathe and timely primrose grow,
Swarth clouds withdrawn (which longer time do tarry)—
    Oh, what is praise, pomp, glory, joy, but so
  As shine by fountains, bubbles, flowers, or snow?

EDMUND BOLTON, in *England's Helicon*, 1600

SAGESSE

LE ciel est, par-dessus le toit,
   Si bleu, si calme!
Un arbre, par-dessus le toit,
   Berce sa palme.

La cloche dans le ciel qu'on voit
   Doucement tinte.
Un oiseau sur l'arbre qu'on voit
   Chante sa plainte.

Mon Dieu, mon Dieu, la vie est là,
   Simple et tranquille.
Cette paisible rumeur-là
   Vient de la ville.

—Qu'as-tu fait, ô toi que voilà
   Pleurant sans cesse,
Dis, qu'as-tu fait, toi que voilà,
   De ta jeunesse?

PAUL VERLAINE
Sagesse, 1881

PILGRIMAGE

Give me my scallop-shell of quiet,
My staff of faith to walk upon,
My scrip of joy, immortal diet,
My bottle of salvation,
My gown of glory, hope's true gage;
And thus I'll take my pilgrimage.

Blood must be my body's balmer;
No other balm will there be given;
Whilst my soul, like a quiet palmer,
Travels towards the land of heaven;
Over the silver mountains,
Where spring the nectar fountains;
And there I'll kiss
The bowl of bliss;
And drink my eternal fill
On every milken hill.
My soul will be a-dry before,
But after, it will ne'er thirst more.

SIR WALTER RALEIGH, in
Diaphantus, 1604

DEATH IN LEAMINGTON

SHE died in the upstairs bedroom
   By the light of the evening star
That shone through the plate glass window
   From over Leamington Spa.

Beside her the lonely crochet
   Lay patiently and unstirred,
But the fingers that would have worked it
   Were dead as the spoken word.

And Nurse came in with the tea-things
   Breast high 'mid the stands and chairs—
But Nurse was alone with her own little soul
   And the things were alone with theirs.

She bolted the big round window,
   She let the blinds unroll,
She set a match to the mantle,
   She covered the fire with coal.

And 'Tea!' she said in a tiny voice
   'Wake up! It's nearly *five*.'
Oh! Chintzy, chintzy cheeriness,
   Half dead and half alive!

Do you know that the stucco is peeling?
   Do you know that the heart will stop?
From those yellow Italianate arches
   Do you hear the plaster drop?

Nurse looked at the silent bedstead,
　At the gray, decaying face,
As the calm of a Leamington evening
　Drifted into the place.

She moved the table of bottles
　Away from the bed to the wall;
And tiptoeing gently over the stairs
　Turned down the gas in the hall.

JOHN BETJEMAN
Continual Dew, 1937

Now every passion sleeps; desponding Love,
And pining Envy, ever-restless Pride;
An holy calm creeps o'er my peaceful soul,
Anger and mad Ambition's storms subside.

O modest Evening, oft let me appear
A wandering votary in thy pensive train,
Listening to every wildly warbling throat
That fills with farewell notes the darkening plain.

JOSEPH WARTON, from
'Ode to Evening', *Odes*, 1746

Very slowly

Komm sü-sser Tod! Komm sel'ge Ruh! Komm füh-re

mich in Frie-de, Weil ich der Welt bin

mü-de. Ach Komm! Ich wart auf dich,

Komm bald, und füh — re mich, Drück mir die —

Au — gen zu. Komm sel — ge Ruh!

Come, sweet death, come heavenly rest!
Come, lead me away in peace,
For I am weary of this world.
Oh come! I wait for thee—
Come soon, come take me,
Close thou mine eyes,
Come, heavenly rest!

WORDS ANONYMOUS, 1725: MELODY AND FIGURED BASS BY JOHN SEBASTIAN BACH, 1736
THE FREE TRANSLATION AND MUSICAL TRANSCRIPTION PREPARED FOR THIS VOLUME

THE WORLD OF LIGHT

THEY are all gone into the world of light!
    And I alone sit lingering here;
Their very memory is fair and bright,
    And my sad thoughts doth clear . . .

I see them walking in an air of glory,
    Whose light doth trample on my days:
My days, which are at best but dull and hoary,
    Mere glimmering and decays.

O holy Hope! and high Humility,
    High as the heavens above!
These are your walks, and you have showed them me,
    To kindle my cold love . . .

If a star were confined into a tomb,
    Her captive flames must needs burn there;
But when the hand that locked her up gives room,
    She'll shine through all the sphere.

O Father of eternal life, and all
    Created glories under Thee!
Resume Thy spirit from this world of thrall
    Into true liberty.

Either disperse these mists, which blot and fill
    My pèrspective still as they pass:
Or else remove me hence unto that hill
    Where I shall need no glass.

HENRY VAUGHAN
Silex Scintillans, Part II, 1655

THE SOUL VISITING THE MANSIONS OF THE DEAD
WATER-COLOUR DRAWING BY PAUL NASH 1932

THE JESTER : FIFTEENTH–CENTURY FLEMISH FIGURE IN BRASS

LIFE IS A JEST

King Death was a rare old fellow
  He sat where no sun could shine,
And he lifted his hand so yellow,
  And poured out his coal black wine.
   Hurrah! for the coal black wine.

There came to him many a maiden,
  Whose eyes had forgot to shine,
And widows with grief o'er laden,
  For a draught of his coal black wine.
   Hurrah! for the coal black wine.

The scholar left all his learning,
  The poet his fancied woes,
And the beauty her bloom returning,
  Like life to the fading rose.
   Hurrah! for the coal black wine.

All came to the rare old fellow,
  Who laughed till his eyes dropped brine,
And he gave them his hand so yellow,
  And pledged them in Death's black wine.
   Hurrah! for the coal black wine.

ANONYMOUS
Nineteenth-century Ballad

VICTORY BELLS

SWEET funeral bells from some incalculable distance, wailing over the dead that die before the dawn, awakened me as I slept in a boat moored to some familiar shore . . .

I sat, and wept in secret the tears that men have ever given to the memory of those that died before the dawn, and by the treachery of earth, our mother. But suddenly the tears and funeral bells were hushed by a shout as of many nations, and by a roar as from some great king's artillery, advancing rapidly along the valleys, and heard afar by echoes from the mountains. 'Hush!' I said, as I bent my ear earthwards to listen—'hush!—this either is the very anarchy of strife, or else'—and then I listened more profoundly, and whispered as I raised my head—'or else, oh heavens! it is *victory* that is final, victory that swallows up all strife.'

THOMAS DE QUINCEY
'The English Mail Coach', in *Blackwood's*, 1849

VITAL spark of heavenly flame!
Dost thou quit this mortal frame?
Trembling, hoping, lingering, flying,
Oh the pain, the bliss of dying!
Cease, fond Nature, cease thy strife,
Let me languish into life.

ALEXANDER POPE, in
Miscellaneous Poems by Several Hands, 1730

170

THE GLORY THAT WE KNEW

Who shall invoke when we are gone
   The glory that we knew?
Can we not carve To-Day in stone,
   In diamond this Dawn's dew?

The song that heart to heart has sung
   Write fadeless on the air;
Expression in eyes briefly hung
   Fix in a planet's stare?

Alas, all beauty flies in Time
   And only as it goes
Upon death's wind its fleeting chime
   Into sad memory blows.

Is this but presage of re-birth
   And of another Day
When what within our hearts we said
   We once again shall say?

Oh no! we never could repeat
   Those numbered looks we gave;
But some pure lustre from their light
   All future worlds shall have.

W. J. TURNER, 'Tragic Love',
Songs and Incantations, 1936

171

THE SOUL'S GARMENT

GREAT Nature clothes the soul, which is but thin,
With fleshly garments, which the Fates do spin;
And when these garments are grown old and bare,
With sickness torn, Death takes them off with care,
And folds them up in peace and quiet rest,
And lays them safe within an earthly chest:
Then scours them well and makes them sweet and clean,
Fit for the soul to wear those clothes again.

MARGARET CAVENDISH, DUCHESS OF NEWCASTLE
Poems and Fancies, 1653

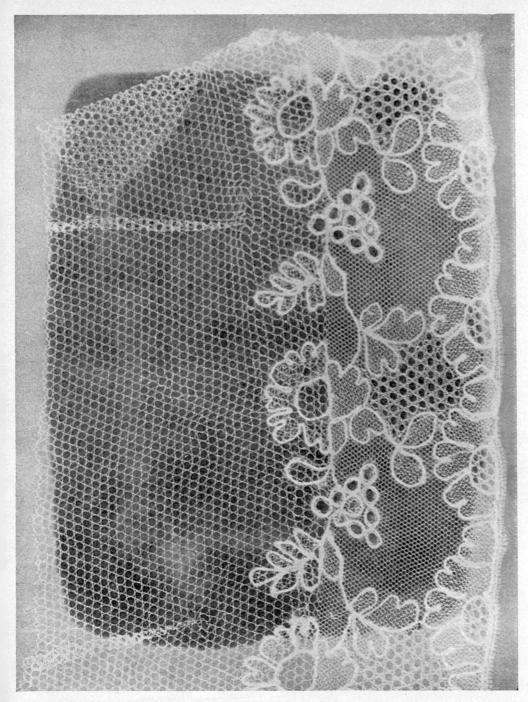

LACE : EARLY VICTORIAN PHOTOGRAPH BY W. H. FOX TALBOT

THE STARRY NIGHT : PAINTING BY VINCENT VAN GOGH 1889

PART TWO: LOOK AT THE STARS!

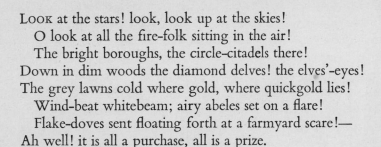

Look at the stars! look, look up at the skies!
  O look at all the fire-folk sitting in the air!
  The bright boroughs, the circle-citadels there!
Down in dim woods the diamond delves! the elves'-eyes!
The grey lawns cold where gold, where quickgold lies!
  Wind-beat whitebeam; airy abeles set on a flare!
  Flake-doves sent floating forth at a farmyard scare!—
Ah well! it is all a purchase, all is a prize.

Buy then! Bid then!—What?—Prayer, patience, alms, vows.
Look, look! a May-mess, like on orchard boughs!
  Look! March-bloom, like on mealed-with-yellow sallow!
These are indeed the barn: within-doors house
The shocks. This piece-bright paling shuts the spouse
  Christ home, Christ and his mother and all his hallows.

GERARD MANLEY HOPKINS
Poems, 1918 (written 1877)

To express hope by some star, the eagerness of a soul by a sunset radiance. Certainly there is nothing in that of stereoscopic realism, but is it not something that actually exists?

VINCENT VAN GOGH

I

THE SEARCH FOR THE FARTHER THING

MAN doth seek a triple perfection: first a sensual, consisting in those things which very life itself requireth either as necessary supplements, or as beauties and ornaments thereof; then an intellectual, consisting in those things which none underneath man is either capable of or acquainted with; lastly a spiritual and divine, consisting in those things whereunto we tend by supernatural means here, but cannot here attain unto them. They that make the first of these three the scope of their whole life are said by the Apostle to have no god but only their belly, to be earthly minded men. Unto the second they bend themselves, who seek especially to excel in all such knowledge and virtue as doth most commend men. To this branch belongeth the law of moral and civil perfection. That there is somewhat higher than either of these two, no other proof doth need than the very process of man's desire, which being natural should be frustrate, if there were not some farther thing wherein it might rest at the length contented, which in the former it cannot do. For man doth not seem to rest satisfied, either with fruition of that wherewith his life is preserved, or with performance of such actions as advance him most deservedly in estimation; but doth further covet, yea often-times manifestly pursue with great sedulity and earnestness, that which cannot stand him in any stead for vital use; that which exceedeth the reach of sense; yea somewhat above capacity of reason, somewhat divine and heavenly, which with hidden exultation it rather surmiseth than conceiveth; somewhat it seeketh, and what that is directly it knoweth not, yet very intentive desire thereof doth so incite it, that all other known delights and pleasures are laid aside, they give place to the search of this but only suspected desire.

RICHARD HOOKER
The Laws of Ecclesiastical Polity, 1594

THE TRIUMPH OF HARMONY

ALL we have willed or hoped or dreamed of good, shall exist;
Not its semblance, but itself; no beauty, nor good, nor power
Whose voice has gone forth, but each survives for the melodist,
When eternity affirms the conception of an hour.
The high that proved too high, the heroic for earth too hard,
The passion that left the ground to lose itself in the sky,
Are music sent up to God by the lover and the bard;
Enough that he heard it once: we shall hear it by and by.

And what is our failure here but a triumph's evidence
For the fullness of the days? Have we withered or agonized?
Why else was the pause prolonged but that singing might issue
    thence?
Why rush the discords in, but that harmony should be prized?
Sorrow is hard to bear, and doubt is slow to clear,
Each sufferer says his say, his scheme of the weal and woe:
But God has a few of us whom he whispers in the ear;
The rest may reason and welcome; 'tis we musicians know.

ROBERT BROWNING, from
'Abt Vogler', *Dramatis Personae*, 1864

THE GEMLIKE FLAME

EVERY moment some form grows perfect in hand or face; some tone on the hills or the sea is choicer than the rest; some mood of passion or insight or intellectual excitement is irresistibly real and attractive for us—for that moment only. Not the fruit of experience, but experience itself, is the end. A counted number of pulses only is given to us of a variegated, dramatic life. How may we see in them all that is to be seen in them by the finest senses? How shall we pass most swiftly from point to point, and be present always at the focus where the greatest number of vital forces unite in their purest energy? To burn always with this hard, gemlike flame, to maintain this ecstacy, is success in life . . . While all melts under our feet, we may well catch at any exquisite passion, or any contribution to knowledge that seems by a lifted horizon to set the spirit free for a moment, or any stirring of the senses, strange dyes, strange colours, and curious odours, or work of the artist's hands . . .

WALTER PATER
Studies on the History of the Renaissance, 1873

'Rubbish', thought Winter—until thrifty Spring
Stitched up the boot with green, and made the kettle sing.

LAURENCE WHISTLER
Engraved by him on the foot of the glass
illustrated opposite

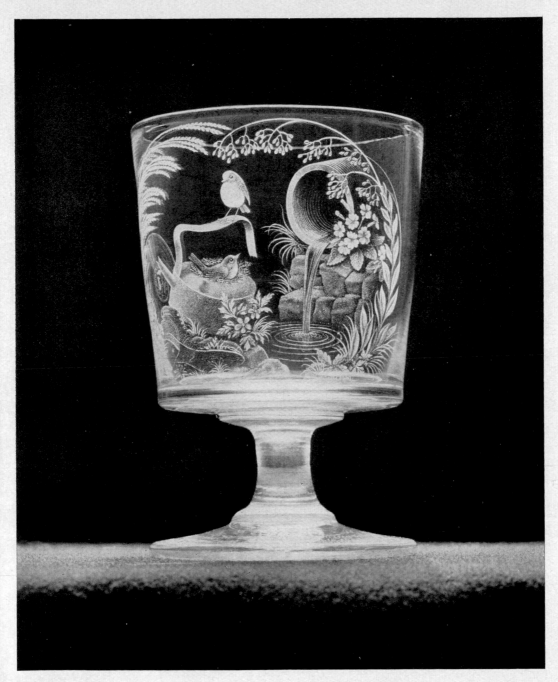

DIAMOND-POINT ENGRAVING ON GLASS : BY LAURENCE WHISTLER 1951

THE ORRERY: PAINTING BY JOSEPH WRIGHT OF DERBY 1766

THE MOTION OF THE SPHERES

I SAW eternity the other night
Like a great ring of pure and endless light,
    All calm, as it was bright;
And, round beneath it, time, in hours, days, years,
    Driven by the spheres,
Like a vast shadow moved, in which the world
    And all her train were hurled.

HENRY VAUGHAN, from
'The World', in *Silex Scintillans*, 1650

REASON

When in the reason's philosophy the rational appears dominant and sole possessor of the world, we can only wonder what place would be left to it, if the element excluded might break through the charm of the magic circle, and, without growing rational, could find expression. Such an idea may be senseless, and such a thought may contradict itself, but it serves to give voice to an obstinate instinct. Unless thought stands for something that falls beyond mere intelligence, if 'thinking' is not used with some strange implication that never was part of the meaning of the word, a lingering scruple still forbids us to believe that reality can ever be purely rational. It may come from a failure in my metaphysics, or from a weakness of the flesh which continues to blind me, but the notion that existence could be the same as understanding strikes as cold and ghost-like as the dreariest materialism. That the glory of this world in the end is appearance leaves the world more glorious, if we feel it is a show of some fuller splendour; but the sensuous curtain is a deception and a cheat, if it hides some colourless movement of atoms, some spectral woof of impalpable abstractions, or unearthly ballet of bloodless categories. Though dragged to such conclusions, we cannot embrace them. Our principles may be true, but they are not reality. They no more *make* that Whole which commands our devotion, than some shredded dissection of human tatters is that warm and breathing beauty of flesh which our hearts found delightful.

FRANCIS HERBERT BRADLEY
The Principles of Logic, 1883

INTELLECT

THE awful shadow of some unseen Power
　　Floats though unseen among us,—visiting
　　This various world with as inconstant wing
As summer winds that creep from flower to flower,—
Like moonbeams that behind some piny mountain shower,
　　It visits with inconstant grace
　　Each human heart and countenance;
Like hues and harmonies of evening,—
　　Like clouds in starlight widely spread,—
　　Like memory of music fled,—
　　Like aught that for its grace may be
Dear, and yet dearer for its mystery.

PERCY BYSSHE SHELLEY
from 'Hymn to Intellectual Beauty'
in *The Examiner*, 1817

BODY AND SOUL

WHAT sweet contentments doth the soul enjoy by the senses? They
are the gates and windows of its knowledge, the organs of its delight . . . If two pilgrims, which have wandered some few miles
together, have a heart's grief when they are near to part, what must
the sorrow be at the parting of two so loving friends and never-
loathing lovers, as are the body and soul?

WILLIAM DRUMMOND of Hawthornden
The Cypresse Grove, 1623

183

HORIZONS I

THE first range of hills, that encircles the scanty vale of human life, is the horizon for the majority of its inhabitants. On its ridges the common sun is born and departs. From them the stars rise, and touching them they vanish. By the many, even this range, the natural limit and bulwark of the vale, is but imperfectly known. Its higher ascents are too often hidden by mists and clouds from uncultivated swamps, which few have courage or curiosity to penetrate. To the multitude below these vapours appear, now as the dark haunts of terrific agents, on which none may intrude with impunity; and now all aglow, with colours not their own, they are gazed at as the splendid palaces of happiness and power. But in all ages there have been a few who, measuring and sounding the rivers of the vale at the feet of their furthest inaccessible falls, have learned that the sources must be far higher and far inward; a few, who even in the level streams have detected elements which neither the vale itself nor the surrounding mountains contained or could supply. How and whence to these thoughts, these strong probabilities, the ascertaining vision, the intuitive knowledge may finally supervene, can be learnt only by the fact. I might oppose to the question the words with which Plotinus suppose Nature to answer a similar difficulty. 'Should any one interrogate her, how she works, if graciously she vouchsafe to listen and speak, she will reply, it behoves thee not to disquiet me with interrogatories, but to understand in silence, even as I am silent, and work without words.'

SAMUEL TAYLOR COLERIDGE
Biographia Literaria, 1817

HORIZONS II

I AM endlessly yearning
To be in Ch'ang-an.
Insects hum of autumn by the gold brim of the well;
A thin frost glistens like little mirrors on my cold mat;
The high lantern flickers; and deeper grows my longing.
I lift the shade and, with many a sigh, gaze upon the moon,
Single as a flower, centred from the clouds.
Above, I see the blueness and deepness of sky.
Below, I see the greenness and the restlessness of water.
Heaven is high, earth wide; bitter between them flies my sorrow.
Can I dream through the gateway, over the mountain?
Endless longing
Breaks my heart.

LI PO, translated by Witter Bynner
from the text of Kiang Kang-hu

ENJOYMENT

You never enjoy the world aright, till the Sea itself floweth in your veins, till you are clothed with the heavens, and crowned with the stars: and perceive yourself to be the sole heir of the whole world and more than so, because men are in it who are everyone sole heirs as well as you. Till you can sing and rejoice and delight in God, as misers do in gold, and Kings in sceptres, you can never enjoy the world.

Till your spirit filleth the whole world, and the stars are your jewels; till you are as familiar with the ways of God in all ages as with your walk and table: till you are intimately acquainted with that shady nothing out of which the world was made: till you love men so as to desire their happiness, with a thirst equal to the zeal of your own: till you delight in God for being good to all: you never enjoy the world. Till you more feel it than your private estate, and are more present in the hemisphere, considering the glories and the beauties there, than in your own house; till you remember how lately you were made, and how wonderful it was when you came into it: and more rejoice in the palace of your glory, than if it has been made but today morning.

THOMAS TRAHERNE, *Centuries of Meditation*, 1908
(written *c.* 1670)

WIND

MAKE me thy lyre, even as the forest is:
What if my leaves are falling like its own!
The tumult of thy mighty harmonies

Will take from both a deep, autumnal tone.
Sweet though in sadness. Be thou, Spirit fierce,
My spirit! Be thou me, impetuous one!

Drive my dead thoughts over the universe
Like withered leaves to quicken a new birth!
And, by the incantation of this verse,

Scatter, as from an unextinguished hearth
Ashes and sparks, my words among mankind!
Be through my lips to unawakened earth

The trumpet of a prophecy! O, Wind,
If Winter comes, can Spring be far behind?

PERCY BYSSHE SHELLEY,
from 'Ode to the West Wind'
Prometheus Unbound, 1820

LIGHT

FIRST-BORN of Chaos, who so fair didst come
    From the old Negro's darksome womb,
    Which, when it saw the lovely child,
The melancholy mass put on kind looks and smiled . . .

Say, from what golden quivers of the sky
    Do all thy wingëd arrows fly?
    Swiftness and power by birth are thine:
From thy great sire they came, thy sire the word divine . . .

Swift as light thoughts their empty career run,
    Thy race is finished when begun:
    Let a post-angel start with thee,
And thou the gaol of earth shalt reach as soon as he . . .

All the world's bravery that delights our eyes
    Is but thy several liveries:
    Thou the rich dye on them bestowest,
Thy nimble pencil paints this landscape as thou goest . . .

Through the soft ways of heaven and air and sea,
    Which open all their pores to thee,
    Like a clear river thou dost glide
And with thy living stream through the close channels slide.

But, where firm bodies thy free course oppose,
    Gently thy source the land o'erflows,
    Takes there possession, and does make,
Of colours mingled, light, a thick and standing lake.

ABRAHAM COWLEY, from
'Hymn to Light', *Works*, 1668

RHAM CASTLE, SUNRISE : PAINTING BY J. M. W. TURNER *c.* 1830

SILVER CHAMBER-STICK WITH SNUFFER-STAND : JOHN BARNARD 1697

NIGHT

SWIFTLY walk o'er the western wave,
    Spirit of Night!
Out of the misty eastern cave
Where, all the long and lone daylight,
Thou wovest dreams of joy and fear
Which make thee terrible and dear—
    Swift be thy flight!

Wrap thy form in a mantle gray,
    Star in-wrought;
Blind with thin hair the eyes of Day;
Kiss her until she be wearied out;
Then wander o'er city and sea and land,
Touching all with thine opiate wand—
    Come, long-sought!

When I arose and saw the dawn,
    I sighed for thee:
When light rode high, and the dew was gone,
And noon lay heavy on flower and tree,
And the weary Day turned to his rest,
Lingering like an unloved guest,
    I sighed for thee.

Thy brother Death came, and cried:
    Wouldst thou me?
Thy sweet child Sleep, the filmy-eyed,
Murmured like a noontide bee:
Shall I nestle near thy side?
Wouldst thou me?—And I replied
    No, not thee!

Death will come when thou art dead,
    Soon, too soon!
Sleep will come when thou art fled.
Of neither would I ask the boon
I ask of thee, belovëd Night—
Swift be thine approaching flight,
    Come soon, soon!

PERCY BYSSHE SHELLEY
Posthumous Poems, 1824 (written 1821)

ENTER these enchanted woods,
    You who dare.
Nothing harms beneath the leaves,
More than waves a swimmer cleaves.
Toss your heart up with the lark,
Foot at peace with mouse and worm,
    Fair you fare.
Only at a dread of dark
Quaver, and they quit their form:
Thousand eyeballs under hoods
    Have you by the hair.
Enter those enchanted woods
    You who dare.

GEORGE MEREDITH, from
'The Woods of Westermain',
Poems and Lyrics of the Joy of Earth, 1883

THE MIDNIGHT SKATERS

THE hop-poles stand in cones,
  The icy pond lurks under,
The pole-tops steeple to the thrones
  Of stars, sound gulfs of wonder;
But not the tallest there, 'tis said,
Could fathom to this pond's black bed.

Then is not death at watch
  Within those secret waters?
What wants he but to catch
  Earth's heedless sons and daughters?
With but a crystal parapet
Between, he has his engines set.

Then on, blood shouts, on, on,
  Twirl, wheel and whip above him,
Dance on this ball-floor thin and wan,
  Use him as though you love him;
Court him, elude him, reel and pass,
And let him hate you through the glass.

EDMUND BLUNDEN
English Poems, 1925

FLOWERS OF NIGHT

Children of night! unfolding meekly, slowly
To the sweet breathings of the shadowy hours,
When dark blue heavens look softest and most holy,
And glow-worm light is in the forest bowers;
    To solemn things and deep,
    To spirit-haunted sleep,
    To thoughts, all purified
    From earth, ye seem allied;
      O dedicated flowers!

Ye, from the gaze of crowds your beauty veiling,
Keep in dim vestal urns the sweetness shrined;
Till the mild moon, on high serenely sailing,
Looks on you tenderly and sadly kind.
    So doth love's dreaming heart
    Dwell from the throng apart,
    And but to shades disclose
    The inmost thought which glows
      With its pure heart entwined.

Shut from the sounds wherein the day rejoices,
To no triumphant song your petals thrill,
But send forth odours with the faint, soft voices
Rising from hidden streams, when all is still.
    So doth lone prayer arise,
    Mingling with secret sighs,
    When grief unfolds, like you,
    Her breast, for heavenly dew
      In silent hours to fill.

FELICIA DOROTHEA HEMANS, *Works,* 1839

THE NIGHT-BLOWING CEREUS : MEZZOTINT FROM 'THE TEMPLE OF FLORA' 1807

THE WATERFALL OF YORO : WOODCUT BY HOKUSAI *c.* 1827

WATER

NOTHING is lovelier than moving water,
The diamond element, innumerable jewel,
Brittle and splintering under the sharp sun,
Yet softer than doves' feathers, and more smooth
Than down of swan.

Nothing is lovelier than water lying still,
When the Moon takes that stillness for her glass.

GERALD BULLETT
Poems in Pencil, 1937

THE RIVER AND THE SEA

I DO not know much about gods; but I think that the river
Is a strong brown god—sullen, untamed and intractable,
Patient to some degree, at first recognized as a frontier;
Useful, untrustworthy, as a conveyor of commerce;
Then only a problem confronting the builder of bridges.
The problem once solved, the brown god is almost forgotten
By the dwellers in cities—ever, however, implacable,
Keeping his seasons and rages, destroyer, reminder
Of what men choose to forget. Unhonoured, unpropitiated
By worshippers of the machine, but waiting, watching and waiting
His rhythm was present in the nursery bedroom,
In the rank ailanthus of the April dooryard,
In the smell of grapes on the autumn table,
And the evening circle in the winter gaslight.

The river is within us, the sea is all about us;
The sea is the land's edge also, the granite
Into which it reaches, the beaches where it tosses
Its hints of earlier and other creation:
The starfish, the hermit crab, the whale's backbone;
The pools where it offers to our curiosity
The more delicate algae and the sea anemone.
It tosses up our losses, the torn seine,
The shattered lobsterpot, the broken oar
And the gear of foreign dead men. The sea has many voices,

Many gods and many voices.

The salt is on the briar rose,

The fog is in the fir trees.

The sea howl

And the sea yelp, are different voices
Often together heard: the whine in the rigging,
The menace and caress of wave that breaks on water,
The distant rote in the granite teeth,
And the wailing warning from the approaching headland
Are all sea voices, and the heaving groaner
Rounded homewards, and the seagull:
And under the oppression of the silent fog
The tolling bell
Measures time not our time, rung by the unhurried
Ground swell, a time
Older than the time of chronometers, older
Than time counted by anxious worried women
Lying awake, calculating the future,
Trying to unweave, unwind, unravel,
And piece together the past and the future,
Between midnight and dawn, when the past is all deception,
The future futureless, before the morning watch
When time stops and time is never ending;
And the ground swell, that is and was from the beginning,
Clangs
The bell.

T. S. ELIOT, from
The Dry Salvages, 1941

199

MOUNTAINS

THE glory of a cloud—without its wane;
  The stillness of the earth—but not its gloom;
The loveliness of life—without its pain;
  The peace—but not the hunger—of the tomb!
Ye Pyramids of God! around whose bases
  The sea foams noteless in his narrow cup;
  And the unseen movements of the earth send up
A murmur which your lulling snow effaces
Like the deer's footsteps. Thrones imperishable!
About whose adamantine steps the breath
Of dying generations vanisheth,
Less cognizable than clouds; and dynasties,
  Less glorious and more feeble than the array
Of your frail glaciers, unregarded rise,
  Totter and vanish. In the uncounted day,
When earth shall tremble as the trump unwraps
  Their sheets of slumber from the crumbling dead,
And the quick, thirsty fire of judgment laps
  The loud sea from the hollow of his bed—
Shall not your God spare *you*, to whom He gave
  No share nor shadow of man's crime, or fate;
  Nothing to render, nor to expiate;
Untainted by his life—untrusted with his grave?

JOHN RUSKIN, 'The Alps, seen
from Marengo', in *The Keepsake*, 1845

ALPINE LANDSCAPE : PAINTING BY JOHN BRETT 1856

WILLY LOTT'S COTTAGE : PAINTING BY JOHN CONSTABLE 1824

THE PEASANT POET

He loved the brook's soft sound
   The swallow swimming by.
He loved the daisy-covered ground,
   The cloud-bedappled sky.

To him the dismal storm appeared
   The very voice of God;
And when the evening rack was reared
   Stood Moses with his rod.

And everything his eyes surveyed,
   The insects in the brake
Were creatures God Almighty made,
   He loved them for His sake—

A silent man in life's affairs,
   A thinker from a boy,
A peasant in his daily cares,
   A poet in his joy.

JOHN CLARE, *Poems,* 1920
(written before 1864)

A GREEN THOUGHT

WHAT wondrous life in this I lead!
Ripe apples drop about my head;
The luscious clusters of the vine
Upon my mouth do crush their wine;
The nectarine and curious peach
Into my hands themselves do reach;
Stumbling on melons, as I pass,
Ensnared with flowers, I fall on grass.

Meanwhile the mind, from pleasure less,
Withdraws into its happiness;
The mind, that ocean where each kind
Does straight its own resemblance find;
Yet it creates, transcending these,
Far other worlds, and other seas;
Annihilating all that's made
To a green thought in a green shade.

Here at the fountain's sliding foot,
Or at some fruit-tree's mossy root,
Casting the body's vest aside,
My soul into the bough does glide;
There, like a bird, it sits and sings,
Then whets and combs its silver wings,
And, till prepared for longer flight,
Waves in its plumes the various light.

ANDREW MARVELL, from 'The Garden'
Miscellaneous Poems, 1681 (written before 1653)

THE BIRDS

NAY more, the very birds of the air, those that be not Hawks, are both so many and so useful and pleasant to mankind, that I must not let them pass without some observations. They both feed and refresh him; feed him with their choice bodies, and refresh him with their heavenly voices. I will not undertake to mention the several kinds of Fowl by which this is done, and his curious palate pleased by day, and which with their very excrements afford him a soft lodging at night. These I will pass by, but not those little nimble musicians of the air, that warble forth their curious ditties, with which nature hath furnished them, to the shame of art.

As first the Lark, when she means to rejoice, to cheer herself and those that hear her; she then quits the earth, and sings as she ascends higher into the air, and, having ended her heavenly employment, grows then mute and sad to think she must descend to the dull earth, which she would not touch, but for necessity.

How do the Blackbird and Thrassle, with their melodious voices, bid welcome to the cheerful Spring, and in their fixed months warble forth such ditties as no art or instrument can reach to!

Nay, the smaller birds also do the like in their particular seasons, as namely the Laverock, the Tit-lark, and the little Linnet, and the honest Robin, that loves mankind both alive and dead.

But the Nightingale, another of my airy creatures, breathes such sweet loud music out of her little instrumental throat, that it might make mankind to think miracles are not ceased. He that at midnight, when the very labourer sleeps securely, should hear, as I have very often, the clear airs, the sweet descants, the natural rising and falling, the doubling and redoubling of her voice, might well be lifted above earth, and say, 'Lord, what music hast thou provided for the Saints in Heaven, when thou affordest bad men such music on earth!'

IZAAK WALTON, *The Compleat Angler*, 1653

A GRAIN OF WHEAT

IF you will look at a grain of wheat you will see that it seems folded up: it has crossed its arms and rolled itself up in a cloak, a fold of which forms a groove, and so gone to sleep. If you look at it some time, as people in the old enchanted days used to look into a mirror, or the magic ink, until they saw living figures therein, you can almost trace a miniature human being in the oval of the grain. It is narrow at the top, where the head would be, and broad across the shoulders, and narrow again down towards the feet; a tiny man or woman has wrapped itself round about with a garment and settled to slumber. Up in the far north, where the dead ice reigns, our arctic explorers used to roll themselves in a sleeping-bag like this, to keep the warmth in their bodies against the chilliness of the night. Down in the south, where the heated sands of Egypt never cool, there in the rock-hewn tombs lie the mummies wrapped and lapped and wound about with a hundred yards of linen, in the hope, it may be, that spices and balm might retain within the sarcophagus some small fragment of human organism through endless ages, till at last the gift of life revisited it. Like a grain of wheat the mummy is folded in its cloth. And I do not know really whether I might not say that these little grains of English corn do not hold within them the actual flesh and blood of man.

RICHARD JEFFERIES
Field and Hedgerow, 1889

ALL'S IN THIS FLOWER

ALL'S in this flower: the war of life and death,
God's character and purpose written down,
The force of love, the proofs and power of faith,
All's here, and all unknown.

Times, seasons, losses, all the fruits of woe,
Beauty's fragility, and death's bare gain,
All plucked in passing by, five minutes ago.
To please a lover that was pleased in vain.

FRANK KENDON, *Tristram*, 1934

To see a world in a grain of sand
And a heaven in a wild flower,
Hold infinity in the palm of your hand
And eternity in an hour.

WILLIAM BLAKE,
from 'Auguries of Innocence', *c.* 1803

THE HUSBANDMAN AND HIS TREES

HUSBANDMAN: Methinks ye swagger and are very brave this May morning, in your beautiful blossoms and green leaves. Whence had ye all this gallantry?

FRUIT-TREES: It pleased our bountiful Creator to bestow it upon us; but it is for thee, and for the sake of mankind which engageth thee, and all men, to acknowledge it, and to serve Him and praise Him with more cheerfulness. This is our language and lesson to all men, which every particular tree among us does daily speak aloud.

HUSBANDMAN: But I have seen you meanly clothed sometimes in the year. I perceive ye change your garments now and then. Have ye several suits of apparel?

FRUIT-TREES: Yes, we are diversely clothed: we wear out a new shirt every year. Our bountiful Lord and Master puts upon us a fresh new garment every spring of the year, and we are very beautiful to look upon all the spring and summer, with various coloured blossoms, leaves and fruits; but towards autumn this brave clothing loseth its fresh colour because the sun, the efficient cause of our springing, growth and flourishing, withdraws from us, and is gone towards the south parts. And as cold weather comes on, these our beautiful garments of leaves and fruits fade and fall from us, by little and little, till we are quite naked; and then, for a season, we are in a melancholy posture . . .

HUSBANDMAN: Ye have many visitors, frequently. Have you this familiar discourse with every one as we have at present, and as often as we are disposed?

FRUIT-TREES: Many people, of all sorts, come from time to time, and walk among us, and look upon us, and commend us for brave, handsome trees, lovely and beautiful, especially when we are in our gallantries full of beautiful blossoms and pleasant and wholesome fruits; and some greedily pluck us, and tear us, and sometimes break off some of our branches to get our fruits, and so go on their ways, but never speak a word with us, neither do they understand what we say to them . . .

HUSBANDMAN: Come, my friends, let us walk into this pleasant garden and have some further discourse with those innocent, harmless companions, the fruit-trees. They will bid us welcome and are still ready and at leisure to confer with us . . . But we must not forget what hath often been said concerning the way and the manner of their discourse with men: that it is not audible to the outward sense of hearing, in the sound of words, but always to the inward sense, the mind and understanding.

RALPH AUSTEN
A Dialogue . . . between the
Husbandman and Fruit-Trees, 1676

A CONTEMPLATION UPON FLOWERS

BRAVE flowers—that I could gallant it like you,
　　And be as little vain!
You come abroad, and make a harmless show,
　　And to your beds of earth again.
You are not proud: you know your birth:
For your embroidered garments are from earth.

You do obey your months and times, but I
　　Would have it ever Spring:
My fate would know no Winter, never die,
　　Nor think of such a thing.
O that I could my bed of earth but view
And smile, and look as cheerfully as you!

O teach me to see Death and not to fear,
　　But rather to take truce!
How often have I seen you at a bier,
　　And there look fresh and spruce!
You fragrant flowers! then teach me, that my breath
Like yours may sweeten and perfume my death.

HENRY KING, BISHOP OF CHICHESTER
British Museum MS. Harl. 6917
(written before 1630)

FLOWER PIE
PAINTING BY JAN DAVIDZ DE HE

LEAVES : PHOTOGRAPH BY EDWIN SMITH

THE SENSIBILITY OF LEAVES

THERE is an exquisite sensibility among the leaves. They do not grow each to his own liking, till they run against one another, and then turn back sulkily; but by a watchful instinct, far apart, they anticipate their companion's courses, as ships at sea, and in every new unfolding of their edged tissue, guide themselves by the sense of each other's remote presence, and by a watchful penetration of leafy purpose in the far future. So that every shadow which one casts on the next, and every touch which in toss of storm each received from the next, aid or arrest the development of their advancing form, and direct, as will be safest and best, the curve of every fold and the current of every vein.

The balance of the bough of a tree is quite as subtle as that of a figure in motion. It is a balance between the elasticity of the bough and the weight of leaves, affected in curvature, literally, by the growth of every leaf; and, besides this, when it moves, it is partly supported by the resistance of the air, greater or less, according to the shape of the leaf;—so that branches float on the wind more than they yield to it; and in their tossing do not so much bend under a force, as rise on a wave, which penetrates in liquid threads through all their sprays.

JOHN RUSKIN
Modern Painters, 1843-60

THE DARKLING THRUSH

I LEANT upon a coppice gate
    When Frost was spectre-gray,
And Winter's dregs made desolate
    The weakening eye of day.
The tangled bine-stems scored the sky
    Like strings of broken lyres,
And all mankind that haunted nigh
    Had sought their household fires.

The land's sharp features seemed to be
    The Century's corpse outleant,
His crypt the cloudy canopy,
    The wind his death-lament.
The ancient pulse of germ and birth
    Was shrunken hard and dry,
And every spirit upon earth
    Seemed fervourless as I.

At once a voice arose among
    The bleak twigs overhead
In a full-hearted evensong
    Of joy illimited;
An aged thrush, frail, gaunt, and small,
    In blast-beruffled plume,
Had chosen thus to fling his soul
    Upon the growing gloom.

So little cause for carolings
   Of such ecstatic sound
Was written on terrestial things
   Afar or nigh around,
That I could think there trembled through
   His happy good-night air
Some blessed Hope, whereof he knew
   And I was unaware.

THOMAS HARDY
Poems of the Past and the Present, 1901

MUSIC COMES

Music comes
Sweetly from the trembling string
When wizard fingers sweep
Dreamily, half asleep;
When through remembering reeds
Ancient airs and murmurs creep,
Oboe oboe following,
Flute answering clear high flute,
Voices, voices—falling mute,
And the jarring drums.

At night I heard
First a waking bird
Out of the quiet darkness sing . . .

Music comes
Strangely to the brain asleep!
And I heard
Soft, wizard fingers sweep
Music from the trembling string,
And through remembering reeds
Ancient airs and murmurs creep;
Oboe oboe following,
Flute calling clear high flute,
Voices faint, falling mute,
And low jarring drums;
Then all those airs
Sweetly jangled—newly strange,
Rich with change . . .
Was it the wind in the reeds?
Did the wind range
Over the trembling string;
Into flute and oboe pouring
Solemn music; sinking, soaring
Low to high,
Up and down the sky?
Was it the wind jarring
Drowsy far-off drums?

Strangely to the brain asleep
Music comes.

JOHN FREEMAN, *Stone Trees*, 1916

A CONCERT OF MUSIC : FULDA PORCELAIN GROUP *c.* 1775

THE MUSIC MASTER: PAINTING BY JAN STEEN c. 1656

HARMONY

IT is my temper, and I like it the better, to affect all harmony; and sure there is music even in the beauty and the silent note which Cupid strikes, far sweeter than the sound of an instrument. For there is a music wherever there is a harmony, order or proportion: and thus far we may maintain the music of the spheres; for those well ordered motions and regular paces, though they give no sound unto the ear, yet to the understanding they strike a note most full of harmony. Whosoever is harmonically composed delights in harmony; which makes me much distrust the symmetry of those heads which declaim against all church-music. For myself, not only from my obedience, but my particular genius, I do embrace it; for even that vulgar and tavern-music, which makes one man merry, another mad, strikes in me a deep fit of devotion, and a profound contemplation of the first Composer. There is something in it of divinity more than the ear discovers: it is an hieroglyphical and shadowed lesson of the whole world, and creatures of God—such a melody to the ear, as the whole world, well understood, would afford the understanding. In brief, it is a sensible fit of that harmony which intellectually sounds in the ears of God.

SIR THOMAS BROWNE
Religio Medici, 1642 (written 1635)

SONG

My soul is an enchanted boat,
Which, like a sleeping swan, doth float
Upon the silver waves of thy sweet singing;
And thine doth like an angel sit
Beside the helm conducting it,
Whilst all the winds with melody are ringing.
It seems to float ever, for ever,
Upon that many-winding river,
Between mountains, woods, abysses,
A paradise of wildernesses!
Till, like one in slumber bound,
Borne to the ocean, I float down, around,
Into a sea profound, of ever-spreading sound:

Meanwhile thy spirit lifts its pinions
In music's most serene dominions;
Catching the winds that fan that happy heaven.
And we sail on, away, afar,
Without a course, without a star,
But, by the instinct of sweet music driven;
Till through Elysian garden islets
By thee, most beautiful of pilots,
Where never mortal pinnace glided,
The boat of my desire is guided:
Realms where the air we breathe is love,
Which in the winds and on the waves doth move,
Harmonizing this earth with what we feel above.

PERCY BYSSHE SHELLEY
from *Prometheus Unbound*, 1820

POETRY

ALL high poetry is infinite; it is as the first acorn, which contained all oaks potentially. Veil after veil may be undrawn, and the inmost naked beauty of the meaning never exposed . . .

Poetry is indeed something divine. It is at once the centre and circumference of knowledge; it is that which comprehends all science, and that to which all science must be referred . . . It is the perfect and consummate surface and bloom of all things; it is as the odour and the colour of the rose to the texture of the elements which compose it, as the form and splendour of unfaded beauty to the secrets of anatomy and corruption . . .

Poetry is not like reasoning, a power to be exerted according to the determination of the will. A man cannot say, 'I will compose poetry.' The greatest poet even cannot say it; for the mind in creation is as a fading coal, which some invisible influence, like an inconstant wind, awakens to transitory brightness; this power arises from within, like the colour of a flower which fades and changes as it is developed, and the conscious portions of our natures are un-prophetic either of its approach or its departure . . .

Poetry . . . is as it were the interpenetration of a diviner nature through our own; but its footsteps are like those of a wind over the sea, which the coming calm erases, and whose traces remain only, as on the wrinkled sand which paves it . . .

Poetry redeems from decay the visitations of the divinity in man.

PERCY BYSSHE SHELLEY
A Defense of Poetry, 1821

THE GARDENS OF THE MUSES

LET thy master, Squire, offer his service to the Muses. It is long since they received any into their court. They give alms continually at their gate, that many come to live upon; but few have they ever admitted into their palace. There shall he find secrets not dangerous to know, sides and parties not factious to hold, precepts and commandments not penal to disobey. The gardens of love wherein he now playeth himself are fresh to-day and fading to-morrow, as the sun comforts them or is turned from them. But the gardens of the Muses keep the privilege of the golden age; they ever flourish and are in league with time. The monuments of wit survive the monuments of power: the verses of a poet endure without a syllable lost, while states and empires pass many periods. Let him not think he shall descend, for he is now upon a hill as a ship is mounted upon the ridge of a wave; but that hill of the Muses is above tempests, always clear and calm; a hill of the goodliest discovery that man can have, being a prospect upon all the errors and wanderings of the present and former times. Yea, in some cliff it leadeth the eye beyond the horizon of time, and giveth no obscure divinations of times to come. So that if he will indeed lead *vitam vitalem*, a life that unites safety and dignity, pleasure and merit; if he will win admiration without envy; if he will be in the feast and not in the throng, in the light and not in the heat; let him embrace the life of study and contemplation.

FRANCIS BACON, BARON VERULAM
Essex's Device, 1595

A YOUNG MAN WRITING : PERSIAN MINIATURE DRAWING

SELF—PORTRAIT : PAINTING BY GEORGE ROMNEY 1782

THE PAINTER

                        You've seen the world
—The beauty and the wonder and the power,
The shapes of things, their colours, lights and shades,
Changes, surprises—and God made it all!
—For what? Do you feel thankful, ay or no,
For this fair town's face, yonder river's line,
The mountain round it and the sky above,
Much more the figures of man, woman, child,
These are the frame to? What's it all about?
To be passed o'er, despised? or dwelt upon,
Wondered at? Oh, this last of course—you say.
But why not do as well as say—paint these
Just as they are, careless what comes of it?
God's works—paint any one, and count it crime
To let a truth slip. Don't object, 'His works
Are here already; nature is complete:
Suppose you reproduce her—(which you can't)
There's no advantage! You must beat her, then.'
For, don't you mark? we're made so that we love
First when we see them painted, things we have passed
Perhaps a hundred times nor cared to see;
And so they are better, painted—better to us,
Which is the same thing. Art was given for that;
God uses us to help each other so,
Lending our minds out.

                ROBERT BROWNING, from
                'Fra Lippo Lippi', *Men and Women,* 1885

NATURE AND ART

NATURE contains the elements, in colour and form, of all pictures, as the keyboard contains the notes of all music.

But the artist is born to pick, and choose, and group with science, these elements, that the result may be beautiful—as the musician gathers his notes, and forms his chords, until he bring forth from chaos glorious harmony . . .

When the evening mist clothes the riverside with poetry, as with a veil, and the poor buildings lose themselves in the dim sky, and the tall chimneys become campanili, and the warehouses are palaces in the night, and the whole city hangs in the heavens, and fairy-land is before us—then the wayfarer hastens home; the working man and the cultured one, the wise man and the one of pleasure, cease to understand, as they have ceased to see, and Nature, who, for once, has sung in tune, sings her exquisite song to the artist alone, her son and her master—her son in that he loves her, her master in that he knows her.

To him her secrets are unfolded, to him her lessons have become gradually clear. He looks at her flower, not with the enlarging lens, that he may gather facts for the botanist, but with the light of the one who sees in her choice selection of brilliant tones and delicate tints, suggestions of future harmonies.

He does not confine himself to purposeless copying, without thought, each blade of grass, as commended by the inconsequent, but, in the long curve of the narrow leaf, corrected by the straight tall stem, he learns how grace is wedded to dignity, how strength enhances sweetness, that elegance shall be the result.

In the citron wing of the pale butterfly, with its dainty spots of orange, he sees before him the stately halls of fair gold, with their slender saffron pillars, and is taught how the delicate drawing high upon the walls shall be traced in tender tones of orpiment, and repeated by the base in notes of graver hue . . .

Through his brain, as through the last alembic, is distilled the refined essence of that thought which began with the Gods, and which they left him to carry out.

Set apart by them to complete their works, he produces that wondrous thing called the masterpiece, which surpasses in perfection all that they have contrived in what is called Nature; and the Gods stand by and marvel, and perceive how far away more beautiful is the Venus of Melos than was their own Eve.

JAMES MCNEILL WHISTLER
The Gentle Art of Making Enemies, 1890

IF the painter wishes to see enchanting beauties, he has the power to produce them. If he wishes to see monstrosities, whether terrifying, or ludicrous and laughable, or pitiful, he has the power and authority to create them. If he wishes to produce towns or deserts, if in the hot season he wants cool and shady places, or in the cold season warm places, he can make them. If he wants valleys, if from high mountain-tops he wants to survey vast stretches of country, if beyond he wants to see the horizon on the sea, he has the power to create all this; and likewise, if from deep valleys he wants to see high mountains or from high mountains deep valleys and beaches. Indeed, whatever exists in the universe, whether in essence, in act, or in the imagination, the painter has first in his mind and then in his hands. His hands are of such excellence that they can present to our view simultaneously whatever well-proportioned harmonies real things exhibit piece-meal.

LEONARDO DA VINCI, *Notebooks*

THE PICTURESQUE

'I PERCEIVE', said Mr. Milestone, after they had walked a few paces, 'these grounds have never been touched by the finger of taste'.

'The place is quite a wilderness,' said Squire Headlong . . .

'My dear Sir,' said Mr. Milestone, 'accord me your permission to wave the wand of enchantment over your grounds. The rocks shall be blown up, the trees shall be cut down, the wilderness and all its goats shall vanish like mist. Pagodas and Chinese bridges, gravel walks and shrubberies, bowling-greens, canals, and clumps of larch, shall rise upon its ruins. One age, Sir, has brought to light the treasures of ancient learning; a second has penetrated into the depths of metaphysics; a third has brought to perfection the science of astronomy: but it was reserved for the exclusive genius of the present times to invent the noble art of picturesque gardening, which has given, as it were, a new tint to the complexion of nature, and a new outline to the physiognomy of the universe!'

'Give me leave,' said Sir Patrick O'Prism, 'to take an exception to that same. Your system of levelling, and trimming, and clipping, and docking, and clumping, and polishing, and cropping, and shaving, destroys all the beautiful intricacies of natural luxuriance, and all the graduated harmonies of light and shade, melting into one another, as you see them on that rock over yonder. I never saw one of your improved places, as you call them, and which are nothing but big bowling-greens, like sheets of green paper, with a parcel of round clumps scattered over them like so many spots of ink, flicked at random out of a pen, and a solitary animal here and there looking as if it were lost, that I did not think it was for all the world like Hounslow Heath, thinly sprinkled over with bushes and highway-men.'

'Sir,' said Mr. Milestone, 'you will have the goodness to make a distinction between the picturesque and the beautiful.'

'Will I?' said Sir Patrick: 'Och! but I won't. For what is beautiful? That what pleases the eye. And what pleases the eye? Tints variously broken and blended. Now, tints variously broken and blended constitute the picturesque.'

'Allow me,' said Mr. Gall. 'I distinguish the picturesque and the beautiful, and I add to them, in the laying out of grounds, a third and distinct character, which I call unexpectedness.'

'Pray, Sir,' said Mr. Milestone, 'by what name do you distinguish this character, when a person walks round the grounds for the second time?'

THOMAS LOVE PEACOCK
Headlong Hall, 1816

No effort to create an impossible or purely ideal landscape is made in the Japanese garden. Its artistic purpose is to copy faithfully the attractions of a veritable landscape, and to convey the real impression that a real landscape communicates. It is therefore at once a picture and a poem; perhaps even more a poem than a picture. For as nature's scenery, in its varying aspects, affects us with sensations of joy or of solemnity, of grimness or of sweetness, of force or of peace, so must the true reflection of it in the labour of the landscape gardener create not merely an impression of beauty, but a mood in the soul.

LAFCADIO HEARN
Glimpses of Unfamiliar Japan, 1894

How can he get wisdom that holdeth the plough, and that glorieth in the goad; that driveth oxen, and is occupied in their labours, and whose talk is of bullocks?

He giveth his mind to make furrows: and is diligent to give the kine fodder.

So every carpenter and work-master, that laboureth night and day: and they that cut and grave seals, and are diligent to make great variety, and give themselves to counterfeit imagery, and watch to finish a work.

The smith also, sitting by the anvil, and considering the iron work, the vapour of the fire wasteth his flesh, and he fighteth with the heat of the furnace: the noise of the hammer and the anvil is ever in his ears, and his eyes look still upon the pattern of the thing that he maketh; he setteth his mind to finish his work, and watcheth to polish it perfectly.

So doth the potter sitting at his work, and turning the wheel about with his feet, who is always carefully set at his work: and maketh all his work by number.

He fashioneth the clay with his arm, and boweth down his strength before his feet; he applieth himself to lead it over; and he is diligent to make clean the furnace.

All these trust to their hands: and every one is wise in his work.

Without these cannot a city be inhabited: and they shall not dwell where they will, nor go up and down.

They shall not be sought for in public counsel, nor sit high in the congregation: they shall not sit on the judge's seat, nor understand the sentence of judgement: they cannot declare justice and judgement, and they shall not be found where parables are spoken.

But they will maintain the state of the world, and all their desire is in the work of their craft.

Ecclesiasticus, xxxviii

THAT thing which I understand by real art is the expression by man of pleasure in labour.

WILLIAM MORRIS

WE may talk what we please of Lilies and Lions Rampant, and Spread Eagles in Fields d'Or or d'Argent; but if Heraldry were guided by Reason, A Plough in a Field Arable would be the most Noble and Antient Armes.

FRANCIS BACON, BARON VERULAM

THE MIGHTY HEART

EARTH has not anything to show more fair:
Dull would he be of soul who could pass by
A sight so touching in its majesty:
This City now doth, like a garment, wear
The beauty of the morning; silent, bare,
Ships, towers, domes, theatres, and temples lie
Open unto the fields, and to the sky;
All bright and glittering in the smokeless air.
Never did sun more beautifully steep
In his first splendour, valley, rock, or hill;
Ne'er saw I, never felt, a calm so deep!
The river glideth at his own sweet will;
Dear God! the very houses seem asleep;
And all that mighty heart is lying still!

WILLIAM WORDSWORTH
Composed on Westminster Bridge, Sept. 3, 1802
Poems, 1807

D WESTMINSTER BRIDGE : PAINTING BY SAMUEL SCOTT *c.* 1750

THE HEAVEN-ASSAILING SPIRES

WITH these heaven-assailing spires
All that was in clay or stone
Fabled of rich Babylon
By these children is outdone.

Earth has spilt her fire in these
To make them of her mightier kind;
Has she that precious fire to give,
The starry-pointing Magian mind,

That soared from the Chaldean plains
Through zones of mystic air, and found
The Master of the Zodiac,
The Will that makes the Wheel go round?

GEORGE WILLIAM RUSSELL (A.E.)
Vale and Other Poems, 1931

THE DREAMING SPIRES

BEAUTIFUL city! so venerable, so lovely, so unravaged by the fierce intellectual life of our century, so serene! 'There are our young barbarians, all at play!' And yet, steeped in sentiment as she lies, spreading her gardens to the moonlight, and whispering from her towers the last enchantments of the Middle Age, who will deny that Oxford, by her ineffable charm, keeps ever calling us nearer to the true goal of all of us, to the ideal, to perfection—to beauty in a word, which is only truth seen from another side?—nearer perhaps than all the science of Tübingen. Adorable dreamer, whose heart has been so romantic! who hast given thyself so prodigally, given thyself to sides and to heroes not mine, only never to the Philistines! Home of lost causes, and forsaken beliefs, and unpopular names, and impossible loyalties!

MATTHEW ARNOLD
Essays in Criticism, 1865

TEARS IN THE STRAND

I HAVE passed all my days in London, until I have formed as many and intense local attachments as any of you mountaineers can have done with dead nature. The lighted shops of the Strand and Fleet Street, the innumerable trades, tradesmen and customers, coaches, waggons, playhouses, all the bustle and wickedness round about Covent Garden, the very women of the Town, the watchmen, drunken scenes, rattles—life awake, if you awake, at all hours of the night, the impossibility of being dull in Fleet Street, the crowds, the very dirt and mud, and sun shining upon houses and pavements, the print shops, the old book-stalls, parsons cheap'ning books, coffee houses, steams of soups from kitchens, the pantomimes, London itself a pantomime and masquerade,—all these things work themselves into my mind and feed me, without a power of satiating me. The wonder of these sights impells me into night-walks about her crowded streets, and I often shed tears in the Motley Strand from fulness of joy at so much life.

CHARLES LAMB
Letter to William Wordsworth
30 January, 1801

PIED BEAUTY

GLORY be to God for dappled things—
For skies of couple-colour as a brinded cow;
For rose-moles all in stipple upon trout that swim;
Fresh-firecoal chestnut-falls; finches' wings;
Landscape plotted and pieced—fold, fallow, and plough;
And all trades, their gear and tackle and trim.

All things counter, original, spare, strange;
Whatever is fickle, freckled (who knows how?)
With swift, slow; sweet, sour; adazzle, dim;
He fathers-forth whose beauty is past change;
            Praise him.

GERARD MANLEY HOPKINS
Poems, 1918 (written 1877)

COWS AT COOKHAM : PAINTING BY STANLEY SPENCER 1936

DEW ON A COBWEB AND PASSION FLOWER : PHOTOGRAPH BY CLARENCE PONTING

THE WEB AND THE DEW

SHALL we, that are but worms, but silk-worms, but glow-worms at the best, chide God that he hath made slow-worms and other venomous creeping things? Shall we, that are nothing but boxes of poison in ourselves, reprove God for making toads and spiders in the world?

JOHN DONNE

ALMOST any man may, like the spider, spin from his own inwards his own airy Citadel. The points of leaves and twigs on which the spider begins her work are few, and she fills the air with a beautiful circuiting. Man should be content with as few points to tip with the fine web of his soul, and weave a tapestry empyrean—full of symbols for his spiritual eye, of softness for his spiritual touch, of space for his wandering, of distinctness for his luxury.

JOHN KEATS
Letter, 19 February, 1818

THE world globes itself in a drop of dew. The microscope cannot find the animalcule which is less perfect for being little . . . So do we put our life into every act. The true doctrine of omnipresence is that God reappears with all his parts in every moss and cobweb.

RALPH WALDO EMERSON, from 'Compensation',
Essays, 1841

M

THE GLORY

THE glory of the beauty of the morning—
The cuckoo crying over the untouched dew;
The blackbird that has found it, and the dove
That tempts me on to something sweeter than love;
White clouds ranged even and fair as new-mown hay;
The heat, the stir, the sublime vacancy
Of sky and meadow and forest and my own heart:—
The glory invites me, yet it leaves me scorning
All I can ever do, all I can be,
Beside the lovely of motion, shape, and hue,
The happiness I fancy fit to dwell
In beauty's presence. Shall I now this day
Begin to seek as far as heaven, as hell,
Wisdom or strength to match this beauty, start
And tread the pale dust pitted with small dark drops,
In hope to find whatever it is I seek,
Hearkening to short-lived happy-seeming things
That we know naught of, in the hazel copse?
Or must I be content with discontent
As larks and swallows are perhaps with wings?
And shall I ask at the day's end once more
What beauty is, and what I can have meant
By happiness? And shall I let all go,
Glad, weary, or both? Or shall I perhaps know
That I was happy oft and oft before,
Awhile forgetting how I am fast pent,
How dreary-swift, with naught to travel to,
Is Time? I cannot bite the day to the core.

EDWARD THOMAS, *Poems*, 1917

NOTES ON THE ILLUSTRATIONS

The names of the owners of works illustrated are printed in italics

Frontispiece JAN VERMEER OF DELFT (1632–75). Allegory of painting. *c.* 1665. Oil on canvas. 47½ × 39¼ in. *Austrian State property.*

It has been supposed that the painter represented is Vermeer himself, but he is clearly intended as a symbol of the creative artist, whilst the model characterizes Fame.

17 DOMENICO THEOTOCOPOULOS, known as EL GRECO (1541–1614). Adoration of Shepherds. 1608. Oil on canvas. 64⅜ × 42⅛ in. *New York, Metropolitan Museum of Art.*

18 ANTONIO ROSSELLINO (1428–78). The Virgin with the laughing Child. *c.* 1465. Statuette in terracotta. 19 in. high. *London, Victoria and Albert Museum.*

This statuette was at one time attributed to Leonardo da Vinci.

25 VAMPIRE JET-FIGHTERS against strato-cumulous clouds. *Picture Post* photograph by Raymond Kleboe. 1950.

26 FRANCIS HAYMAN, R.A. (1708–76). The Masters Martin Atkins. *c.* 1760. Oil on canvas. 30 × 25 in. *Leggatt Brothers.*

In this characteristic portrait-group by an undeservedly neglected painter of the Georgian scene is there not more than a hint of the feeling and technique of his renowned pupil, Thomas Gainsborough?

35 SHELDON TAPESTRY. Summer, one of the Four Seasons. 1611. The illustration shows a little less than half of the complete tapestry, which measures 10 × 12 ft. *The Marquess of Salisbury.*

The Four Seasons, now at Hatfield House, were woven for Ralph Sheldon at his factory in Gloucestershire, and are probably the finest English tapestries of their period in existence.

36 STAFFORDSHIRE POTTERY. Salt-glaze stoneware figure of a horseman, decorated in dark brown. *c.* 1740. 9¼ in. high. *London, Victoria and Albert Museum.*

41 THOMAS GAINSBOROUGH, R.A. (1727–88). The painter's daughters. *c.* 1760. Oil on canvas. 29¾ × 24¾ in. *London, National Gallery, by permission of the Trustees.*

Mary, the elder of Gainsborough's daughters, was born in 1748, made an unhappy marriage, and went mad. Her sister Margaret, born in 1752, was also a queer, abnormal creature. Their childhood, however, appears to have been singularly happy.

42 A MILKMAID. Staffordshire earthenware group, with mottled glazes, *c.* 1755. 8½ in. high. *Cambridge, Fitzwilliam Museum, by permission of the Syndics.*

Perhaps a product of Thomas Whieldon's pottery at Fenton. Milking groups were favourite 'chimney-piece' ornaments in the second half of the eighteenth century. This is one of the earliest and most elaborate of its kind.

47 JEAN ANTOINE WATTEAU (1684–1721). A girl sewing. *c.* 1710. Drawing in black and red chalk. 9 × 6½ in. *The Trustees of the Elvedon Estate.*

48 HENRY WALTON (1746–1813). A pretty maid buying a ballad. 1778. Oil on canvas. 37×29 in. *The Hon. Mrs John White.*

Little known though he is, Walton was a *genre* painter of great accomplishment, with a delicacy of sentiment which lifts his work out of the typical Georgian conventions of his time.

57 ANTONIO ALLEGRI DA CORREGGIO (*c.* 1489–1534). Jupiter and Antiope. *c.* 1522. Oil on canvas. 74¾×48¾ in. *Paris, Musée du Louvre.*

58 FRENCH MIRROR CASE, in ivory. First half of the fourteenth century. 4 in. diameter. *London, Victoria and Albert Museum.*

63 VIVIEN LEIGH, as Cleopatra, in Sir Laurence Olivier's production of *Antony and Cleopatra,* by William Shakespeare. London 1951, New York 1952. Photograph by Angus McBean.

64 RALPH WOOD (1716–72). Shepherd and shepherdess. *c.* 1760. Earthenware group with mottled glazes. 9¼ in. high. *London, Victoria and Albert Museum.*

69 NICHOLAS HILLIARD (1547–1619). A love-sick Courtier. *c.* 1590. Oval miniature painting in water-colours. $5\frac{9}{32} \times 2\frac{13}{16}$ in. *London, Victoria and Albert Museum.*

Inscribed *Dat pœnas laudata fides*—'My praisëd faith procures my pain'. There is a head-and-shoulders portrait by Hilliard of the same young man, aged twenty-two in 1588, in the Metropolitan Museum of Art, New York.

70 THE MILDENHALL TREASURE. The Neptune dish. Roman silver, decorated with two concentric zones of figure ornament in relief, and a centre medallion. Fourth century. Diameter, 1 ft 11¾ in. *London, British Museum, by permission of the Trustees.*

The chief piece in the superb collection of silver table-ware dug up in a field near Mildenhall, Suffolk, in 1946.

79 QUEEN ANNE WALNUT TOILET MIRROR, with early Georgian glass candlestick. *Mrs John Micklem.* Photograph by E. & D. Gibbs, by courtesy of Messrs Phillips of Hitchin.

80 GEORG DIONYSIUS EHRET (1708–70). Rosa Mundi. *c.* 1745. Water-colour drawing on vellum. 11¾ in. high. *London, Victoria and Albert Museum.*

Son of a Heidelberg market gardener, Ehret lived in England from 1736, and his botanical drawings certainly equal, and perhaps surpass, those of the more famous Redouté. *Rosa Mundi* is said to derive its name from Fair Rosamund, the mistress of Henry II.

85 ARTHUR DEVIS (1711–87). Lady Caroline Leigh, angling. *c.* 1744. Oil on canvas. 30 × 24½ in. *Major and the Hon. Mrs R. N. Macdonald-Buchanan.*

86 FRANÇOIS BOUCHER (1703–70). Undine. *c.* 1753. Drawing in coloured chalks. 7⅝ × 10⅞ in. *Paris, Musée du Louvre.*

This drawing of a sea nymph is a study for one of the figures in 'Le Coucher du Soleil' in the Wallace Collection, London.

91 SIMON BARTRAM. Watch in brass case. London, *c.* 1640. Photograph by courtesy of Mr James Oakes, London.

Simon Bartram was one of the petitioners for the incorporation of the Clockmakers' Company, and served as its Master in 1646. The watch illustrated is of the type worn on a chatelaine, before the popularization of the pocket watch. It is unusual to find two hands on a watch as early as this.

92 SIR FRANCIS GRANT, P.R.A. (1803–78). The Lady Sophia Pelham, riding 'Jenny Lind'. 1853. Oil on canvas. 88 × 90 in. *The Earl of Yarborough.*

101 PHILIP WILSON STEER (1860–1942). The Toilet of Venus. 1898. Oil on canvas. 100 × 72 in. *London, Tate Gallery, by permission of the Trustees.*

102 AUGUSTE RODIN (1840–1917). The Kiss. 1886. Sculpture in marble. 75 in. high. *Paris, Musée Rodin.*

107 AFTER CHI'EN HSÜAN (1235–90). A spirit of the waves. Chinese painting on silk. 54¼ × 36½ in. *London, British Museum, by permission of the Trustees.*

108 JAN VAN EYCK (1385–1441). Arnolfini and his bride. 1434. Oil on wooden panel. 33 × 22½ in. *London, National Gallery, by permission of the Trustees.*

This, the greatest picture of its kind and period, was supposedly a record of the marriage of Giovanni Arnolfini and his wife, Jeanne de Cename. The room in which it was painted survived until recently, in a street of Bruges. Arnolfini raises his hand in solemn pledge. The terrier typifies faithfulness, the wooden pattens are set aside to show that the couple stand on holy ground, and the artist, who can be faintly discerned in the mirror at the back, set his signature above it—'Johannes de Eyck fuit hic 1434'—he was indeed 'here', as witness to the marriage which he recorded for all time.

113 HENRY MOORE (born 1898). Madonna and Child. 1943. Sculpture in Hornton stone. 5½ ft. high. *St Matthew's Church, Northampton.*

114 CASPAR NETSCHER (1639–84). Mother and children. Oil on canvas. 21½ × 19 in. *London, Eugene Slatter Gallery.*

This masterpiece of seventeenth-century Dutch interior painting was bought in 1767 by Prince Galitzine, on the advice of Voltaire and Diderot, for Catherine the Great. It became part of the Hermitage Palace Collection in St Petersburg.

123 STAFFORDSHIRE POTTERY GROUP. The tea party. *c.* 1745. Astbury-Whieldon earthenware, with mottled glazes. 6¾ in. high. *A. R. A. Hobson, Esq.*

I know of no group of the period which is comparable with this elaborate 'primitive'. It has never been illustrated before.

124 MARGOT FONTEYN in 'Les Sylphides'. Setting by Nadia Benois. Photograph by Gordon Anthony.

129 PREHISTORIC CAVE PAINTING. A running horse. Aurignacian era, perhaps 20,000 years B.C. 10 ft long. Lascaux, France.

130 BEN MARSHALL (1767–1835). Tom Oldaker, Huntsman of the Berkeley Hounds, on 'Pickle'. 1800. 40×50 in. *Major and the Hon. Mrs R. N. Macdonald-Buchanan.*

135 CHINESE POTTERY FIGURE. Sleeve dancer. T'ang period, 618–906. 8 in. high. *London, British Museum, by permission of the Trustees.*

136 BISHAN DAS AND NANHA. The Garden of Felicity. Mughal miniature painting. *c.* 1590. 8¾ × 5½ in. *London, Victoria and Albert Museum.*

Babar, the first great mogul of India, combined with his ruthless ambitions an intense delight in gardens, one of which is shown in this illustration to his Memoirs. He was as proud of having seen thirty-four different kinds of tulip in India as he was of his military triumphs.

145 JOHN ZOFFANY, R.A. (1733–1810). The Bradshaw family. Oil on canvas. 52×70 in. *E. E. Cook, Esq.*

146 SPARSHOLT CHURCH, BERKSHIRE. Photograph by Edwin Smith.

151 ASCRIBED TO NICHOLAS HILLIARD (1547–1619). Queen Elizabeth. *c.* 1585. Oil on panel. 37½ × 34 in. *The Marquess of Salisbury.*

Known as the 'Ermine' portrait, because of the ermine by the Queen's side, signifying purity, this magnificent portrait has remained in the Cecil family, at Hatfield House, since Elizabethan times. It has not hitherto been reproduced in colour.

152 REMBRANDT VAN RIJN (1606–69). Portrait of an old lady (believed to be Françoise van Wasserhoven). 1634. Oil on panel. 27×21 in. *London, National Gallery, by permission of the Trustees.*

157 JOHN DWIGHT (*c.* 1637–1703). Lydia Dwight. 1673. White saltglaze stoneware figure. 10 in. high. *London, Victoria and Albert Museum.*

Inscribed 'Lydia Dwight dyed March 3, 1673', this portrait of the daughter of the Fulham potter has been attributed speculatively to the young Grinling Gibbons.

158 FRANCESCO GUARDI (1712–93). Classical composition. Oil on canvas. 37×28½ in. *London, Victoria and Albert Museum.*

167 PAUL NASH (1889–1946). The soul visiting the Mansions of the Dead. 1932. Water-colour drawing. 10½ × 6¾ in. *The British Council.*

This drawing was done as an illustration to Sir Thomas Browne's *Urn-Burial* (La Belle Sauvage), though it also has a beautiful affinity to Vaughan's poem.

168 FLEMISH BRASS FIGURE. The jester. Fifteenth century. 13 in. high. *London, Victoria and Albert Museum.*

173 WILLIAM HENRY FOX TALBOT (1800–77). Lace. Photograph. *c.* 1844. 8¼ × 6¼ in.

Originally reproduced in *The Pencil of Nature*, 1844, this is one of the earliest photographs by the discoverer of the calotype process from which photography developed.

174 VINCENT VAN GOGH (1853–90). The Starry Night. 1889. Oil on canvas. 29 × 36¼ in. *New York, The Museum of Modern Art* (acquired through the Lillie P. Bliss Bequest).

179 LAURENCE WHISTLER (b. 1907). Diamond-point engraving on a Georgian rummer. 1951. 5 in. high. *Mrs Eric Raffles.*

Laurence Whistler's engravings on glass certainly equal, perhaps surpass, the finest work of Wolff and Schouman in the eighteenth century. He engraves original verses on many of the glasses which he decorates.

180 JOSEPH WRIGHT, A.R.A., OF DERBY (1734–97). The Orrery. 1766. Oil on canvas. 58 × 80 in. *Derby, Museum and Art Gallery.*

First exhibited at the Royal Academy under the title: 'A Philosopher giving that lecture on the Orrery, in which a lamp is put in place of the sun.'

189 J. M. W. TURNER, R.A. (1775–1851). Norham Castle, Sunrise. *c.* 1830. Oil on canvas. 35⅝ × 47¼ in. *London, Tate Gallery, by permission of the Trustees.*

190 JOHN BARNARD. Silver chamber-stick with snuffer-stand and extinguisher. London hall-mark, 1697. Weight 17 oz. 8 dwt. Photograph by Raymond Fortt, by courtesy of Messrs Thomas Lumley, London.

195 PHILIP REINAGLE (1749–1833) and ABRAHAM PETHER (1756–1812). The night-blowing Cereus. Mezzotint by Dunkarton for Thornton's *Temple of Flora*, 1807. 19 × 14 in.

The 'Queen of the Night' as this cactus was called, was intro-duced from Jamaica in 1700 and became a romantic favourite of Regency gardeners. Its flowers open in the evening, and are fully blown by midnight.

196 HOKUSAI (1760–1849). The Waterfall of Yoro. *c.* 1827. Japanese woodcut. $15\frac{1}{8} \times 10\frac{1}{2}$ in. *London, British Museum, by permission of the Trustees.*

201 JOHN BRETT (1831–1902). Alpine Landscape. 1856. Oil on canvas. 18×15 in. *London, Tate Gallery, by permission of the Trustees.*

Brett, one of the more individual of the Pre-Raphaelites, was a friend of Ruskin, and accompanied him on visits to Switzerland.

202 JOHN CONSTABLE, R.A. (1776–1837). Willy Lott's Cottage. 1824. Oil on paper. $9\frac{1}{2} \times 7$ in. *London, Victoria and Albert Museum.*

A small and not over-familiar study of a favourite subject.

211 JAN DAVIDZ DE HEEM (1606–84). Flower piece. Oil on canvas. 36×28 in. *Mrs Eugene Slatter*

In this floral galaxy—which the artist painted with lavish dis-regard of the seasons—a highly specialized form of art is seen at the peak of achievement—every petal, every leaf, every insect and drop of water microscopically mirrored on the canvas.

212 LEAVES. Photograph by Edwin Smith.

217 FULDA PORCELAIN. A concert of music. Glazed white porcelain. *c.* 1775. 16 in. high. *London, Victoria and Albert Museum.*

The Fulda factory, established under the patronage of the Prince-Bishop, Heinrich von Bibra, produced some of the finest German porcelain, in a material of luminous whiteness.

218 JAN STEEN (1626–79). The music master. *c.* 1656. Oil on wood. 16½ × 12½ in. *London, National Gallery, by permission of the Trustees.*

223 PERSIAN MINIATURE DRAWING. A young man writing. Early seventeenth century. 6 × 3 in. *Wilfrid Blunt, Esq.*

224 GEORGE ROMNEY (1734–1802). Self portrait. 1782. Oil on canvas, unfinished. 49½ × 39 in. *London, National Portrait Gallery, by permission of the Trustees.*

232 SAMUEL SCOTT (1702–72). Old Westminster Bridge. *c.* 1750. Oil on canvas. 11¼ × 21½ in. Vernon Collection. *London, Tate Gallery, by permission of the Trustees.*

The old Westminster Bridge shown here, which was the subject of Wordsworth's poem, was completed in 1750.

233 NEW YORK. Photograph by Ewing Galloway.

239 STANLEY SPENCER (b. 1891). Cows at Cookham. 1936. Oil on canvas. 30 × 20 in. *Thomas Balston, Esq.*

240 DEW ON A COBWEB AND PASSION FLOWER. Photograph by Clarence Ponting.

Endpapers: From a fabric designed by William Morris for Kelmscott House. *c.* 1880. *London, Victoria and Albert Museum.*

INDEX OF AUTHORS AND COMPOSERS